MW01104350

In Search Of The Blue Lotus:

A Feminist Counter-Narrative To The Dominant Hegemonic Discourse

Written By S Sandra Sukhan

Produced by:

FriesenPress
Suite 300 – 852 Fort Street
Victoria, BC, Canada V8W 1H8

www.friesenpress.com

Distributed to the trade by The Ingram Book Company

Dedicated to...

my family – those who are in my life and those who came before me and laid the foundation for my life. To my friends and teachers - those who inspired me and continue to do so. I love you all.

Table of Contents

Acknowledgement

I would like to acknowledge the contributions from my friend Arlene Petkau who did the substantive edits for this book and kept me focused. She provided honest feedback in a gentle and supportive way, making me feel that the stories are worth telling.

I would like to say a special thanks to my husband Robin who, besides doing the proof-reading and editing several times, kept me grounded during my many hours of writing.

If I did not have the many wonderful friends and family to share my life, there would be no stories to tell. I am afraid that I might forget to mention someone who really made a difference so I will thank all of you collectively.

Foreword

Many of us move from childhood to adulthood without much thought about how the events of our childhood might impact our lives. For some of us, those experiences are good and we remember them fondly. For others, those childhood experiences can be quite traumatic, leading us in all kinds of directions, some of which we do not understand because we either do not connect them to our youth or we choose not to remember them because they are too painful. My life was, and is, no different from so many other people's lives. Some memories are happy, some are sad or traumatic. This is my telling of my story. The book is less about me as the storyteller and more about the stories I tell based on the themes that flow through all our lives.

This book was initially written as a chapter in my doctoral dissertation. It is an autoethnographic account of my life experiences. Through a first-person reflexive narrative, I will address my own growing awareness of some of the issues that affected my life – issues such as racism, gender, democracy, freedom, class struggles, hegemony, social class, privileges, unequal power relations, resistance to colonial politics, and ultimately my own complicity in, and efforts to challenge the normative discourse of the dominant ideology. I describe normative discourse as dominant groups in society defining, implicitly or explicitly, what is considered "normal" based on their cultural, political and social values. For example, Canada has a long history of accepting immigrants, but historically, that acceptance was based on how closely one looks like the dominant racial and cultural groups of Western European heritage. In the last few decades, Canada has become much more ethnically diverse, but the reality is that the more closely aligned a new immigrant is to the still-dominant white culture, the easier it is to integrate into that. Levels of education, speaking the same language, being the same race, having the same religious beliefs, having the same sexual preferences, and male dominance are only a few of the ways in which dominant groups systemically exert power. Some cultures who were farther removed tried, to assimilate by changing names, religions or moving to neighbourhoods that were perceived in terms of social class to be more desirable.

To ensure some degree of authenticity of my experiences, I use language and make references to words, phrases or ideas that may not always be clear to a non-Guyanese. I ask the reader's indulgence in this. At times, the diary entries may seem to end abruptly; that is deliberate. It ensures a degree of authenticity similar to my personal diary entries where I do not always write in a manner that is tidy. As the diary unfolds, I will be expressing my own *praxis* – the cycle of action and reflection - using the readings of various authors whose work informs my writing. *Praxis* does not happen in a linear manner, as my experiences in this diary indicate. Some entries are messy and have no resolution at the moment. The answers to some questions may happen years later in a different entry or not at all. Since the book was modified for publication, it does not follow the normal conventions for academic citations and referencing because it is not so much an academic text as it is storytelling.

Introduction

Some background information might be useful to the reader as to why this book was written in the first place. I was accepted into a doctoral program in September 2007. In June 2010, during my dissertation proposal exam, my examining committee, a group with whom I had been working since the start of my doctoral studies, suggested I write another chapter explaining my interest in doing research in vocational education. The committee felt I was in a unique position because of my life experiences and those needed to be documented. They suggested that I use autoethnography to tell the story. I felt self-conscious about asking what autoethnography meant, as it was a word I had not heard of. They explained briefly and suggested some books that I should read on the topic. I was very reluctant to add more work to my already overloaded schedule. At that time, I was one of the primary caregivers for my father who had terminal cancer and I was working and studying full-time. Writing another chapter seemed daunting and overwhelming.

I immediately started reading a few of the books they suggested and searched for academic journal articles on the topic of autoethnography. Every chapter I read made me feel that this was the perfect way to capture all the thoughts that were whirling around in my head for years. I had finally found the name for the thing I was doing without thought - telling my life story - but instead of using the oral tradition which was a cultural norm for me, I would write them down. Autoethnography in this context is my attempt to locate myself via a post-colonial approach within the capitalist culture of vocational education where I have worked for almost 40 years. My experiences are seen through my lenses as a woman of colour working in a traditionally male-dominated area of vocational education which has conventionally focused on training the less privileged working classes for employment. Since research and writing is not value-free, meaning that we all have biases based on experience and perspective, I used reflexive autoethnography as a way of claiming my own personal agency documenting my experiences, and laying bare my own biases and subjectivities.

Reed-Danahay[1] describes autoethnography as a form of narrative where you incorporate elements of your life experiences and place those within a social context because you have first-hand knowledge of the culture about which you write, thus lending authority to that which you witnessed. This genre of writing and research, as described by Ellis and Bochner,[2] connects the personal and cultural through multi-layered consciousness. Spry[3] points out that autoethnography is less about a confessional tale and more about weaving story and theory. The theory I was studying in this case was about critical pedagogy which is based on the themes that I previously mentioned and how they affect vocational teacher training. For me, it was a way of combining historical research and educational practice as suggested by Wexler[4].

Epistemologically, I believe that my autoethnographic accounts diverge from the positivist representations of what are considered data in vocational education because often times, such representations focus on quantitative data such as how many students entered a program, how many left without completing the program, how many found work related to their training and how much they are getting paid. I wanted to focus on the social dimensions of vocational teacher training and how we can better prepare those teachers to deal with the challenges they face daily in the classroom that are not related to the content they teach. Kincheloe[5] suggests that a critically reflective theory of knowledge is an attempt to move beyond the oversimplification and distortions of some scientific knowledge.

By the end of June, 2010, I made the decision to write the autoethnographic chapter and use it as a research method that complements the themes of critical pedagogy which I was studying, writing and teaching. No sooner did I make the decision to write the chapter than I sat at my computer and felt that every thought I had ever had about my life came pouring out onto the pages. I wrote at a fast, furious pace and within four weeks, I had so much material that the chapter was more than twice the length of the other chapters. I sent the draft to my academic advisor with a note saying that writing the chapter was cathartic in many ways but the document was already twice as long as the other chapters and I still had so much that was left unwritten. She read the chapter, said she was delighted with it and advised me to keep writing. I could save the entire chapter for possible publication at a later date but I could remove some of the content for the dissertation. In the end, none of what I had written to that point was removed but I did not add more, feeling that I had much more to say, leaving what was unwritten for a later time. This is that time.

By writing this, I realize I am making myself vulnerable to critique or criticism as autoethnography can often be subject to misinterpretation. Some of my experiences are troubling and painful. As previously stated, drawing upon my personal details such as social background, age, gender, ethnicity, education, qualifications, work experience, and skills allows me to be self-reflexive about the role of "self" in a research project, that is: my personal beliefs, my personal interests in the area of investigation, my experiences linked to the topic of the research and my expertise in relation to the topic. Since my life and educational experiences from student to tradesperson to scholar have not followed the normal chronological trajectories of life events, it is important for me to map the landscape to my dissertation. This allows the reader to get a sense of the ways my personal experiences have influenced the directions of my research. The events are based on my memories of particular periods of my life, thus the diary is based on my understandings and interpretations of those events.

I keep personal diaries but I do not write in an autoethnographic manner, at least not in a manner that would reflect the autoethnography of vocational education. Therefore, none of this book's entries are excerpted from my actual diaries. They are instead "excerpts" from my memory of my life's events as they unfolded and my eventual understandings of how those events shaped my life's choices. Svensson[6] posits that memory is an important historical part of identity formation; therefore, what and how we remember events are equally important. Heider[7] explains that sometimes ethnographers have different versions of the same story based on some significant attributes such as gender, age, race, family status, personal health, culture and value system, the time period, and the ethnographer's theoretical orientation. He refers to this phenomenon as the Rashomon effect. He postulates that even when "mistakes" are made, it reveals something about the background of the ethnographer as well as the importance to the culture concerned.

The book is organized into four chapters and serves as a reflective diary, starting from my life as a seven-year-old child in 1961 in Guyana, South America (the first period of my life which I can recall) to my present location in Winnipeg, Canada.

The events I write about impacted my personal and professional life in terms of my educational choices, my work as a scholar and my social activism. In writing about growing up in the 1960s, I can see that I had little understanding that I was living through a defining chapter of Guyana's (formerly British Guiana) colonial history. The events of that period helped shape the lives of all British Guianese people, including me. Some of the names have been changed because of the sensitivity of some of the subject matter.

The first chapter of the book is based on my experiences in my formative years (child to mid-teens in Guyana), focused specifically on issues of privilege, power, politics, racism, and gender relations. During that period, my awareness quotient of such issues was nascent but had a huge impact on my later life.

The second chapter focuses on my arrival in Canada as a teenager for an arranged marriage and continuing high school education (young adulthood). It was a period of many changes in my life as a new immigrant, finding myself trying to contend for the first time in a subaltern position with such labels as "coloured," "minority," "exotic," "uncultured," and "daft." It was also a period of my own growing awareness of inequities which I had either never experienced or was not aware of. My growing understanding, at some intuitive level, of my choice to become a hairstylist figured prominently, as I did not realize the implications of choosing such a class-based profession.

The third chapter addresses my years as a university student in my late thirties (a new but older scholar), apparently crossing invisible social class lines I was yet again not aware of, and simultaneously gaining some knowledge and language to start critiquing inequalities at an academic level. This was also a time of growing realization for me. Being engaged in coursework, discussion and teaching about issues of social justice opened doors I had not previously thought of, but ones that created other challenges regarding my hybrid and multiple positionalities as a scholar, an immigrant, and a woman of colour.

The fourth chapter addresses some of the successes and challenges I continue to face as a teacher-educator (academic, scholar, tradesperson). This all comes at a time in my life when I find I have to over-credentialize myself to be taken seriously as a scholar by those who represent the dominant ideology while at the same time, I have to minimize my academic credentials to continue my work as a professional hairstylist. It is also my attempt through autoethnography to resist the dominant discourse by providing my first person counter-narrative.

·1·

≈

1961

Dear diary,

Today me and Bena and Karran played in the backyard and I climbed the tall coconut tree next to the genip tree. You know the one i am talking about. It looked tall when I started but by the time I got to the top it was taller when I looked down. Maybe its 40 feet from the ground or taller even. I shonta climbed that coconut tree because I cut the side of my big toe on the zinc sheet and I know daddy will be angry because he told me before he left for the milk plant today that I should be good. If I hide it from mommy maybe she won't tell daddy but how will I wear my shoes to go to school tomorrow? I think mommy wishes I was a boy because I only want to do boy things like climb the trees and play marbles and cricket. And I am very strong and I don't like to dress up and comb my hair. Does that make me like a boy? Girls just don't do fun things. I am supposed to learn how to cook and clean. Thats no fun. Just because Karran is a boy he gets to go out with the other boys in the neighbourhood and play cricket and marbles all day and I have to do stupid girl things.

Dear diary,

Mr. Jury drives a nice car to work every day. Sometimes when I pass his gate, he waits inside his yard in his car and Tar Baby goes and opens the gate for him and he give Tar Baby a cent or a penny. Tar Baby waits to open the gate for Mr. Jury then he runs to school with the money and buys sugar cakes from Salim. Some of the bigger children said we shouldn't open the gate for Mr. Jury. We should show him that coolie people have rights too and white people can't boss us around. But Mr. Jury is nice and he smiles at me every time. Sometimes I want to tell him my name is Savitree but I'm shy. He is rich and his house is nice and he has lots of servants, one for in his house and one for the garden and one for his children. The servant said that he has a toilet that flushes in his house and she is even allowed to use it even though she is a servant. He doesn't have a latrine like us because white people have flush toilets. But not all white people. Auntie Rosa has a flush toilet too. Mommy says she's not really white but she likes to pretend that she is white because she lived in England with white people and sometimes she could pass for white. Mommy said she is really a fair skinned Portuguese and besides she is mixed with some black that's why her hair is so curly but not like me and daddy because we are pure indians and our curly hair is indian curly hair not black curly hair. I don't know what that means. Why does she want to pass for white? Mommy is almost white and we don't have a flush toilet. People say mommy is like a Putaghee and I think she likes it. I asked her what Putaghee means and she said that she is really fair and could pass for Portuguese. I had to ask mommy to spell that word because some of them are hard to spell.

Dear diary,

Yesterday when I was sitting with Salim helping him sell his sugar cakes at school, I asked him how he got blind. He said he was a baby and he doesn't remember but his mommy said they were poor and couldn't afford to go to the hospital so he got sick at home and one day when he woke up from his sickness, he couldn't see. He calls me his angel but I don't mind because he is blind but if he could see I would tell him not to call me a girl name of angel. He likes when I help him sell at recreation because sometimes the children bring pretend money and give him and that makes me sad. I can see if they give him pretend money and he said that for a girl I'm smart in my sums and can make change quickly. I was excited to go home and tell mommy and daddy that Salim says I am smart because sometimes daddy gets upset if I don't bring first in class in all my subjects.

Dear diary,

Salim doesn't have any kids but he helps take care of his sister's children because they are poor. I didn't tell him that sometimes when I'm helping him sell his sugar cakes, I put my penny into his cup but I don't take two sugar cakes. Sometimes I only put a cent but sometimes if I get more money from daddy, I put a penny. I don't think Salim would like it if I would just give him my money so I don't tell him. I am sad that he was blind but I am glad he doesn't see me because he would see that I was giving him money. Is that like cheating if I don't tell him that I'm giving him money? His house is old and when the rain fall, the zinc sheets blow off the roof and his bed gets wet. Last year his mad sister had to come to the backyard to pick up one that blow off. I don't think that happens to Mr. Jury. I never saw Mr. Jury's house inside, only the yard and it looks pretty with all the different colours of flowers. I never went to Salim's house either even though he lives close to our back yard. His mad sister runs off her head and she screams a lot so we are not allowed to go there. They said she should go to the mad house but she doesn't have any money even to go to the mad house. Mad houses are for poor people so i don't know why she has to pay to go there.

1962

Dear diary,

Today is my birthday and I got a going out dress. Now I can take one of my older going out dresses and use it for my afternoon dress. I don't know which one to use for my afternoon dress. And now I have to decide which afternoon dress I will use as a morning dress. Why do we have to have morning clothes and afternoon clothes and going out clothes and school clothes? At least I don't have to use my school uniform at home like some of my friends. Daddy's birthday is tomorrow and mommy made a cake for him and me. I wish I could get my own cake. Bena got a dress like mine too. I know she is my sister and I should be nice but why does she always get a present on my birthday? Every time I get something for my birthday she has to get the same thing too. It's not even her birthday till July 29th. Daddy buys me a present on her birthday too but I don't mind then. It's like having two birthdays every year, one in February and one in July. Sometimes people think we are twins because we dress alike but I'm taller than her and besides I'm one year older. Nelly has to wear her older sister's clothes but Bena doesn't have to wear mine because daddy always buys two – one for her and one for me. Oh diary, guess what, when I went upstairs to get ready for bed, Uncle Boysee was downstairs talking to daddy and he was saying that things could get bad. I was scared because they were almost whispering like he is telling daddy a secret. I was hardly breathing when I was standing so quietly at the top of the step because I didn't want the landing to creak so daddy would know I was listening to him.

Dear diary,

Shanta stays in her school clothes all day and all afternoon even when she is at home. She comes to Auntie Betty's shop after school with her school clothes. She never wears any shoes to school. She is lucky. When it rains she gets to walk barefoot in all the puddles and trenches and me, I have to wear long boots and a rain coat. I'm not allowed to go into the trenches and catch tadpoles after the rain but sometimes I take off my boots and let her wear it and I stick my uniform into my panty legs and go into the trench in front of Uncle Boysee house. I got a long string of tadpoles one day but good thing he doesn't see me or I know he will tell me to get out of the trench and he will tell daddy that I'm walking in the trench and getting my uniform muddy. Shanta says I'm lucky because I get to wear short rubber boots if it's only muddy and long rubber boots if there is a lot of rain. I think she is lucky because she doesn't even have to put on shoes and socks when she goes to school every day. She likes when I let her wear my boots because she can pretend they belong to her. She looks sad when she has to give them back.

Dear diary,

We talked about the day in Big ABC when we had the big flood and Belair school had lots of water in the yard. Shanta had lots of friends that day because her head was wet when she got to school and all the other children were patting her head to get some water to clean their slates. I was jealous because nobody wanted to use my hair to clean their slate because my head was dry. Shanta was crying and she told the teacher that she was cold because her uniform was wet. The teacher said that she should go home and change into a dry uniform but she only had one uniform and her mommy washed it the day before and because it was raining for a lot of days, her uniform didn't dry in time for school even when her mommy pressed it in the morning to dry it, so she had to go to school with the wet uniform. I think it was a good thing that it was raining so that way no one would know if it was wet when she left home but she said that when she put it on, she got cold all day and all night too. I still remember that day even now that I'm 8. Shanta is lucky. She gets biscuits and powder milk that the school is giving away but i don't get any. I lined up with Shanta to get some but Miss Jarvis said I can't have any because I am not poor and daddy works at the milk plant so i can get fresh cow milk anytime I want and mommy can buy biscuit for me at the store because we have money. I think i should get some biscuits too just like the other children. I never get to do what the other children get to do.

Dear dairy,

Things are not good. Daddy said that there is a strike all over the country and the civil servants and workers are not going to work. I don't know what a civil servant is, i think it is some kind of servant that is not rude. Daddy made me look up civil in the dictionary so I think that is a civil servant. We went to school today and the teachers said that they are not striking. I don't know what strike means. I know that when you strike someone you hit them but I don't know what any of this means. They are using words but when I try to put the meaning together, it is not making sense. Mr. Lall's face looked serious so I know it must be bad. Mr. Lall always smiles and pats my shoulder so if he doesn't smile I know that he's sad about something.

Dear diary,

Today was a bad day. I was really scared because everyone at school said that the black people have to move out from Belair because they are going to kill us. The teachers let us go home early and they said not to stop and talk to any black people and if a black man tries to catch us we should scream and run home. I ran all the way home and was crying quietly in the bedroom because I didn't want anyone to know. Sometimes I cry when I am sad or scared but I don't think that is a good thing. When I came out of the bedroom, my face was red and Neighbour asked me what was wrong. I wish my face wouldn't get red like that when I'm scared or happy. Sister Khemo says that because I'm fair skinned, it shows more and I should not be upset. She thinks it looks nice but I hate it.

I told Neighbour that Miss Jarvis sent us home early because some black people want to kill us. I was even more scared because Miss Jarvis is black and if we didn't leave school right away, I think she would kill us. But she plays the piano so nicely when i go to Redeemer church and she sings good too. I don't think piano players are killers but I don't know. Last week at Sunday school they told us to love thy neighbour as thyself. I asked Neighbour why the black people wanted to kill us at school. Didn't they like children? She said that some black people don't like Indian people. But why? I am nice to all my friends. I told Neighbour it's a good thing she is not black. She asked me what I think black means. I said I didn't know but it must mean "bad." Neighbour said that black means "skin colour" not "bad" and she was black. I said that it was okay because I have lots of relatives that are black skinned and she said it wasn't the same thing. She said that black people have black skin and curly hair like steel wool. I said that Uncle Boysee had black skin and curly hair like steel wool. She said it wasn't the same thing. It was race. What does race mean? We have races at school during recreation and most of the time I win because I can run fast. So does that make you bad if you're black skinned and have curly hair like steel wool and you don't bring first in the race? She said no it was about a different kind of race. I don't think I want to hear anymore. I am getting confused when big people talk about hard things. I will just go outside and play some cricket. Neighbour said I have to bathe first and change out of my uniform and into my afternoon clothes and not to get my afternoon clothes ripped because they will have to become my morning clothes. She said that sometimes I am proper careless with my clothes and soon I will have more morning clothes than afternoon clothes and I will look like Dalla the beggaman. I had to wear my slippers to go outside because mommy will be angry that my foot bottom get dirty but I like to walk barefoot even when it hurts sometimes on the hot concrete or bricks or the shells that we brung from the beach to throw in the yard. It makes me feel like the other children. They get to walk barefoot and we have to wear these stupid shoes and slippers.

Dear diary,

Things are getting worse and I am really scared. There are lots of people going to Uncle Boysee house every day. I can see them from my window at school because Miss Jarvis put me to sit there. I think she likes me because she only puts children she likes in the seats close to the windows so we could get lots of breeze when the school gets hot from the midday sun. Tar Baby says it is because I talk too much. I don't think she likes Tar Baby. He has to sit near to her desk and when he doesn't get his sums right, she hits his knuckles with her ruler and sometimes with her wild cane. I feel sorry for him because boys are supposed to be smart at adding but he is a proper dunce. I am smarter than him and Miss Jarvis says that I will pass my Common Entrance exam when I am ten and go to a good school and then she calls him dunce and says that he will fail and have to stay at Belair school and turn into a useless knock-about.

Dear diary,

I was walking to school today with Devika and I saw some men in a van go to Uncle Boysee yard again. I walked faster because I wanted to hear what they were saying. I'm like that diary. I like to know what is going on even if it is none of my business. Sometimes I stand behind my bedroom door and listen to daddy talking to people in the gallery or on the front step. Sometimes I try to say something too but Daddy says that children are to be seen and not heard. I asked him why God gave me a mouth and he said if I gave him any back talk, he would box my mouth. Diary sometimes it is hard to be a little child. One day when I grow up I'll get to talk as much as I want and nobody will stop me. Oh yes dairy, I was telling you how I walked fast to get to Uncle Boysee house. But the men didn't go to Uncle Boysee house. They went to Uncle Mangal house and Uncle Boysee wife was peeping though her window to see what the men were doing. They looked ugly and one of them had some blood on his face and his shirt was ripped. He sat on Uncle Mangal step and he started to hold his head and cry. I didn't think men are allowed to cry. I thought just girls cried. I was silent in school all day thinking about that. Imagine me being silent diary.

Dear diary,

There are lots of men around the road every night and they walk with akya sticks. I hear people calling them vigelanty men. They walk around at night to protect the people in Belair from black people. I asked Daddy how come Mr. Powley is black and he is in the vigelanty group. Daddy said that Mr Powley lived in Belair long enough so he is like family. At night time the men walk around with sticks and sometimes they have cutlasses and they keep watch to make sure that black people don't come to kill us when we sleep. Sometimes I am scared to go to sleep at night so I lay awake and think about what I would do if a thief comes into the house or if a black man comes to kill me. Mommy said that we are safe but I don't feel safe. I am scared all the time but I try not to look like that and mostly I try not to cry. I asked about the vigelanty men and Buddy said that in Buxton there are vigelanty men but they are black and they will chop up Indian men if they catch the Indian men in Buxton. Most people are scared to drive through Buxton because they say black people are dangerous. I think Buddy is trying to make me scared but he said in Bachelors Adventure and Enmore, the vigelanty men are Indian and black people are scared to go there. Diary, I really don't understand all this black people and Indian people talk especially when Mr. Powley is a black man in a vigelanty group with Indian men in belair. I wonder if he would chop up a black man if he comes into Belair to kill us. Sometimes me and Devika walk to school slowly and run home after school because we are scared. Diary, I have to tell you something funny. Sometimes when me and Devika walk home, she shelters in my shadow because she is short and I am so tall. We laugh about it and I try not to walk too fast so that she can get some shade from my shadow. Diary, don't you think that is funny? I am glad I am tall but sometimes my aunty asks daddy what he is feeding me to make me grow so tall because most of the other girls who are my age are short.

1963

Dear diary,

Last night was a terrible night. The sky was red and there was lots of smoke. Buddy said Georgetown is burning. Me and Bena and Karran stand on the back step till late and watched the orange flames in the sky. I was scared to go to bed but I had to go but I didn't sleep all night, i was trembling. I was thinking that I would fall asleep and the flames would reach our house and burn it. I cloaked up next to Bena all night and tried to breathe quietly so that she would not know that I was still awake. The bedroom looked bright all night like it was a full moon and I was glad when it was day break and I could get up. Daytime does not make me as scared. I thought I would stop being scared when I turned 8 but it is now two weeks after my birthday and I'm still scared of some things. I am only telling you this. No one else knows and when I smile a lot people think that I am brave. I am brave most of the time. Will I grow out of being scared? I hope so diary.

Dear diary,

The sky is worse than last night. It was black and red and orange and grey and black cobweb and ashes are floating everywhere. It looks worse than when cane is burning and the black pot from the cane gets in the house and turn everything dirty. The smoke looks like God is angry and he painted the sky in ugly colours. I looked at the Chronicle newspaper and they said yesterday was black Friday because Georgetown was burning. Is that the same as Good Friday? I don't understand what is so good about Good Friday. Palm Sunday seems nicer because we get to cut branches from the coconut trees and decorate the church. Then good Friday everyone is quiet when they go to church and the hymns are sad. If they killed Jesus why is that good? There is nothing good about good Friday.

There was a picture of Uncle Mangal on the front page of the Chronicle with a loud speaker in his hand and beside him was the man who was in his yard crying. They said Uncle Mangal started the fire with his words. I asked daddy what that means because I have to use a match to start a fire. Diary, remember that time when I went to the fowl pen with Bena and Karran and I was trying to smoke the squash vine? I nearly burned off my eyebrows because the vine catch on fire when I sucked in to smoke. Good thing I didn't burn my hair. I stole one of the matches that mommy lights the kerosene stove with and hide it all day. Remember? Daddy said smoking is not good but he smokes and I wanted to try too but I had to do it in secret. Well not a secret exactly if I shared the dry squash vine with Bena and Karran. I was smiling to myself while I was reading the newspaper but it was a good thing daddy didn't see me because he would ask why I was smiling when I was reading something serious.

I have to read the newspaper to him every day so that I can learn to spell big words better and I can do good at dictation in school. Only thing is that I want to stop and ask questions when I don't understand something and then by the time daddy explains it to me I have to start over because I forget what I was reading about. Daddy said that words are dangerous things and people should be careful when they use them. I asked why the newspaper was blaming Uncle Mangal for the fire and daddy said that Uncle Mangal used the loud speaker to instigate the crowd. That was one of the big words in the paper so I copied it in here even though I don't know what it means. I wanted to know more about Uncle Mangal so I didn't ask daddy to explain what instigate means. Besides I know what he would do. He would make me go to the dictionary and find the word and write the meaning on a piece of paper and then I would have to make a sentence with it tomorrow. So I pretended that I already know the word so he wouldn't know that I don't know it. Well he explained that Uncle Mangal stand in front of the electricity corporation with his loud speaker and was shouting <u>attack, attack</u> and a lot of men ran into the compound and set the building on fire and the wind was blowing really hard and the fire went to other buildings and there was only a few fire trucks and they couldn't stop all the fires. He said it was raging. I didn't ask about raging either because I wanted to hear what happened. Daddy said that Uncle Mangal was working at D'Aguar and that's why he joined the Peter D'aguar party that the newspaper called the United Force. The newspaper said that the United Force is trying to disrupt the government. I don't even know what that means but I don't want to ask daddy because it will cost me a lot of work for asking so many questions.

Dear diary,

Auntie Mangal came to our house and she was crying. Daddy told me to go upstairs and I stood at the top of the stairs where he couldn't see me and I listened. She said that Uncle Mangal was going to the airport and he had a gun in the trunk of his car and the police stopped him and arrested him. Auntie Mangal wanted daddy to go to the jail and get uncle Mangal out but daddy said uncle Mangal was at Brickdam police station and it was too dangerous to go there right now. We just call her Auntie because I don't know her name and when I talk about her to Bena I call her Auntie Mangal. Everyone has a name when they are born so how come we call her Auntie Mangal? I should ask about that but I ask too many questions and sometimes mommy gets fed up with answering them. I think that the men who went to his house were planning the fire and maybe the man who was crying didn't want to set the fire. Maybe he had children and didn't want to cause trouble for anyone. I made that up because I don't know why they were at the house so I just pretend that I do. Neighbour says I should tell stories because I have a proper good imagination. I love neighbour. She smells like baby powder and coconut oil.

Dear diary,

Uncle Mangal came out of jail and I think he is hiding at his house for a few days because he didn't come over to our house like he does every day to talk to daddy. Now I have two uncles who went to jail and they both live in the same yard. Uncle Boysee went to jail but it was the year I was born so I don't know much about it. No one talks about that time and I know I'm not allowed to ask because children are not supposed to know some things. Uncle Mangal didn't spend a long time in jail

– maybe a day but his daughter Chandani was crying at school when the other children said she was a jailbird daughter. I want to ask why Uncle Boysee went to jail but diary, sometimes you just know that you cannot ask some things. Cousin Ralph said that some times when he was walking on the road, some of the Belair family shout out jailbird even though it was his father who went to jail.

I wonder if uncle Mangal and his family will still go to the drive-in with us on Tuesday nights. I like Chandani but sometimes I don't want them to go with us because the morris minor is small and can hardly fit ten of us. I always have to have one of the children sitting on my lap and when we get to the drive-in, we all have to sit outside because we can't all fit in the car and listen to the speaker. Daddy said that it is carload night and since uncle Mangal doesn't have a car, we should let he and his children come with us. I like when we go to Brown Betty after the movies and daddy buys ice cream. Uncle Mangal doesn't buy any, even for his children so daddy buys for them too. Maybe he doesn't have enough money to do that or maybe he is stingy. Diary, I don't always know things so I make them up because I don't like not knowing.

Dear diary,

Uncle Mangal came over to our house today and he and daddy were talking. He said those limees suspended the constitution and people civil liberties got taken away.

These days I don't know many of the words that they are saying. It was the same kind of conversation that daddy had with Dr. Jagan when we went to him yesterday to get our teeth checked for holes.

I like Dr Jagan but I don't like the smell of his office. He gives me those glass tubes that the teeth freezing liquid come in and I pull out the plugs and play with them. Daddy says that Dr. Jagan is a good man and he tries to do good things for people but the British government doesn't like him because he is a trouble maker and they think he is a commie. I don't know what a commie is but I hear daddy using it and I see the word on the seawall when we go for walks in the afternoon. I saw the word. I think Dr Jagan is nice so if he is a commie, that's okay.

Uncle Boysee spends a lot of time with him at Freedom House. I would like to go there and see what it looks like inside but children are not allowed. Because how people talk about Freedom House it must be special.

Dr. Jagan's wife is a white lady and she talks kind of different than the other white people who live in British Guiana. People say its because she is from America.

People call her Mrs. Jagan but I know her first name is Janet because sometimes when I go to Uncle Boysee she is visiting and he calls her Janet. Some people in Belair said that her country was glad to see her leave because she is a commie.

Diary, so many words are different these days. I feel like a proper dunce because I try to pay attention when the people are talking with the loud speakers at the rallies by our house but most times I don't know what they are saying.

Sometimes they say things like "free BG" and they chant and shout and raise their hands in the air. But when they hear the police coming, everybody runs away. Sometimes they come and hide upstairs at our house. Uncle Boysee said that if the police catch them, they will have to go to jail. They don't do anything bad. They just shout a lot when the van with the loud speaker comes around and hand out flyers.

I heard Uncle Boysee saying that we have to get freedom from the British but we are not in jail so I don't know if he means that he doesn't want to go back to jail. Uncle Boysee doesn't look like a bad man so I don't know why he went to jail.

Diary, you see how good I am getting at paragraphs? The teachers are teaching us to write in paragraphs so that's why I am using a lot of them today. I don't really know when to use them but I am trying to learn how.

Dear Diary,

I didn't write for almost four months because so many things happened and I was too scared and forgetful to write. The soldiers were all over the place and they had guns and their faces were red. They would come in the land rovers and sometimes they would stop at our house and mommy would give them water. I even know some of them but I don't talk to them. I just give them the jug of water. They spend a lot of time patrolling in Belair now that Cheddi is living here. I'm supposed to call him Dr Jagan but I'm only writing it in here. Good thing daddy doesn't read my diary or he would box me if he knows that I am calling Cheddi by his first name. We have to call all the big people mister or mistress and if they are family we have to say uncle or auntie even if we don't know them. Sometimes the people we call uncle and auntie are not our real uncle or auntie so I don't really know the rules about that.

Cheddi came over to our house last week and asked Daddy if Bena and I could go over and play with his daughter Nadira because she doesn't know too many people in Belair but I don't know what to say to her. Most of my friends I had since I was born and not too many new people come to live in Belair. I went to his house but Nadira was shy and so was I. I didn't talk to her too much. I should go back tomorrow or next week but I don't know what to say. We could play in the bottom house with the empty sardine cans and or I could take her on the train line and we could set some nails on the train line to flatten them and we could make pen knives. I'm not supposed to do that but I don't like that the boys can do that and I can't so I make Bayney take the nail to the train line when the train is coming and he has to flatten it for me or I make sure he doesn't get to climb the guava tree or walk through our yard. Diary sometimes I can be mean but if I don't get mean, the boys don't include me.

Dear diary,

You have to hear this. You know that boy named Kaleem who comes through our yard with Muni and Bayney? Well last week they were passing through with their pellet guns and they sat on the front step and put down the gun. I picked up the gun diary and I shouldn't have done that. When I picked up the gun I was trembling because guns make me scared. I think it's because I see the soldiers with them. I asked Muni if the gun had any pellets and he said they never leave any in the gun. I aimed the gun at the steel gate and pretended that I was shooting the gate and I pulled the trigger. I heard a loud explosion and then Kaleem fell right next to me. I didn't know what happened but later Buddy said that the pellet hit the gate and rickoshayed into Kaleems chest. I nearly killed him and I got even more scared and started to cry. People were screaming and I didn't know what to do. There was blood on his chest and they took him to the hospital in a car. My tummy was hurting very bad and I thought that i am going to get some serious licks but daddy and mommy told me it was an accident. I couldn't sleep because I thought the police would come for me but they didn't come. I know they're going to come this week and lock me up like Uncle Mangal and Uncle Boysee. Even now I want to vomit when I think about it. I start to tremble because I am so scared and my cheeks are hurting because I am forcing myself to smile so no one sees that I am scared

I keep praying every night and I hope God is listening to me. If I had a telephone then I could ask him if he could save me from jail. I told mommy that I didn't want to go to jail and I didn't mean to shoot Kaleem. She said that not everyone who goes to jail is bad. I asked her if she knows any good people who went to jail and maybe I could talk to them. She said Uncle Boysee went to jail but he was trying to do a good thing for us and the British people didn't like that so they put him and Cheddi in jail. She said he was a political prisoner. Maybe I could be a political prisoner because I'm not a bad person.

Dairy these days too many things are happening that I don't understand. I see all kinds of signs that I don't know. Did I tell you about the one in Bobby's yard? It say red China go home. Bobby is Chinese and he doesn't even come from China. He was born in Belair so why do they want him to go back to China? This is his home. And at the seawall I saw lots of signs saying Vote PPP and another one saying PYO and a big one that says Long Live Che. Right next door to Uncle Geoff they found a dead man in a barrel of water. Somebody drowned him but they didn't see who it is. Uncle Geoff said it is a PYO house. Diary I just want to be in Big ABC again and be five. Nine is not so much fun.

1964

Dear Diary,

Daddy and Mommy built this big chicken pen in the yard and we have lots of laying hens. We have to pick up eggs every day and I don't like doing that but we have to do it or the hens will start picking and eating the eggs and when they do that, they spoil all the eggs. Every week we have people coming to see how daddy and mommy set up the chicken coops. We have to put saw dust on the ground and the chicken get water from these long troughs that fill up when the water and food gets too low. It works by itself. The chickens can drink and eat anytime they are thirsty or hungry so we don't have to go and feed them like some people do but we have to go every day and check to make sure that the feeders and water troughs are working. Sometimes the feeders get stuck so I have to shake it to make the feed come down. Sometimes the chickens pick at the auto thing and the water doesn't shut off and then there is a terrible mess because the sawdust gets wet and it smells really bad. Then we have to go and shovel it out in the wheel barrow and dump it in the pit in the backyard.

I really don't like doing all that work but I have to do it. One time, the chickens got sick and every day we get lot of dead ones so we had to kill all of them and burn them in the pit at the back. It smelled like burnt feathers. It was bad. We had to disinfect the coops over and over with some liquid before we could get more chickens.

Daddy and Mommy said that they would not get any more laying hens because now everybody is doing that. So now we have broilers. They buy one day old chicks and we have to keep them warm with some heating lights for a week or two. They are eight week broilers so we sell them after that time. People are always coming to our house to buy chickens. They always ask us when the chickens will be ready. Karran and I are getting good at looking at a chicken to tell how much it weighs. We are selling so much that we must be rich by now. I don't have much time to play with my friends. They think I am lucky to get to eat chickens whenever I want but I hate chickens now. I don't like when I have to put the chickens in the cones and cut off their heads and I don't like the smell of the wet feathers when we have to put the dead chickens in hot water to pluck them so I don't eat any of it.

Dear Diary,

Today we got thousands of baby chicks. I want to keep one or two for pets but mommy says that people don't have chickens for pets. We had to disinfect the chicken coops before the chickens came. We have to spend a lot of time to clean them every day and make sure that the water troughs are not wetting the saw dust. Kwang Hing supermarket is buying lots of chickens from daddy so he had to buy a plucking machine. Mommy has to wear pants to use the machine because one day when she was wearing a dress, it got tangled in the machine and she nearly had a terrible accident. Good thing she reached the switch quickly and shut it off or the machine would have sucked her in. Grandfather Khartoon told daddy that women don't wear pants, that mommy was trying to be a man, especially now that she has a boycut hairstyle. He told daddy to come home and stop mommy from wearing pants because it doesn't look good. Mommy said that he can come and pluck the chickens if he doesn't like her wearing pants.

Those old people are always telling us how to act but I am glad that sometimes mommy doesn't listen. Mostly she listens to him but not this time. She said that she owes him a lot. She said that when she and daddy got married in 1952 and she moved to Belair, none of daddy's relatives talked to her because she was muslim and daddy is hindu. Diary, do you know that my daddy's name is Dood? Dood means milk in Hindi and daddy says that his name suits him because he loves milk. Mommy's name is Shariefan but everyone calls her Babai or Baba. I don't know why. It's not a false name or anything like that. Some people have a right name and a home name and some people only have a right name. Daddy and Mommy call me Sandra because they baptized me with that name at the Lutheran church but everyone else calls me Sav or Savi. That's short for Savitree so I don't have a home name.

So diary I was telling you about how daddy's family didn't want him to marry a muslim woman. They said that Dood is a hindu and he should not marry a muslim. They said that it is against his religion and it is not right to marry someone who is not hindu. And they used to say his wife thinks that she is a white woman wearing shoes all day like white people. They said that she thinks she is too good to go barefoot like them.

So mommy and daddy never got invited at anybody's house. Mommy said that it was hard to be living in Belair and not be invited to anybody's house. After a year, Grandfather Khartoon told the other relatives that mommy was a nice girl and they should welcome her into the family. Then people started being nice to her. That was long before I was born but I am glad that the relatives talk to us even if grandfather Khartoon is a watchman on his veranda. It would be sad to think that I if I said good morning to all those relatives every day that they would not talk to me.

Dear diary,

Kwang Hing only wants the best chickens so we have to pluck the feathers clean and make sure the skins don't tear and then we put them in the right size plastic bags and tie them up nicely. It's a lot of work for us but mommy can do it very good and she is teaching us. We sell the neck and liver and gizzard and head and foot in a different package but not to the supermarket. They only want the best ones because only white people and rich people go and shop there and they don't eat liver and gizzards and necks. Some people come to us to buy the live chicken but a lot of people from Sophia and Gutter Dam and Liliandaal come to buy the head and foot or the liver and gizzard or the necks. Some just get the liver and gizzard because that is cheaper than the live chicken but some people buy only the head and foot because that is more cheap. The people who buy head and foot wear old clothes to come to our house and the people who buy the whole chicken come with nice clothes and slippers. I wouldn't buy any of it. I just like to eat fish these days but some of my friends think that I am spoiled because I have all the chicken I want and I don't want to eat any of it. My stomach feels bad when I smell the chicken. Every time I try to put it in my mouth, it smells like wet feathers.

Dear diary,

Last week we had to pluck about 200 chickens for the super-market. After school, we had to come home and start plucking and it went on almost all night. I was so busy that I could not eat any dinner because I was too tired. We plucked till ten oclock that night and mommy said that I had to go and bathe and go to sleep because I was sleeping while I was plucking the chicken. I was so tired that I did not want to bathe but I smelled like raw chicken and guts so I had to bathe. I leaned up against the wall in the bathroom and I was sleeping. Diary, I hate the smell of chicken and the guts was the worse. Some of the chickens are sick so when I cut them open, they smell terrible and I want to vomit. I wish daddy would sell them and do something else. I never want to eat chicken again. My friends think I am lucky to be able to go to the fowl pen and catch a chicken anytime to eat but I don't feel lucky after plucking so many chickens. I went to school and all I was smelling was chicken blood on my clothes and my hands but my friends said that I smelled like Palmolive soap and baby powder. I smell raw chicken everywhere. Some of the people in belair are building chicken pens to sell chick-ens because they see lots of people coming to our yard to buy chicken, so even when I walk to school it is like all the air in Belair is just smelling like chicken shit everywhere. That's a bad word but I am angry diary. I just want to stop killing the chick-ens and I want to stop putting them in hot water and cleaning the feather but mostly I want to stop cutting them open and pulling out the guts.

Dear diary,

I was thinking about mommy for a while. She is different from a lot of the women in Belair. Most of them have long hair and her hair is very short. The ladies stay home and mommy goes out to work and neighbour takes care of us. Mommy wears very nice clothes. She has alligator skin shoes and she has some high heel slippers with diamonds at the front. Sometimes when she is not at home, I wear her shoes but she knows it because they don't fit me and I twist them. She drives daddy's car and I can see the other ladies looking at her as if they can't understand how daddy is letting her do that. One day when she was learning to drive, she crashed the car into a donkey cart and daddy was upset but he did the same thing when he went to fill up the car at a petrol station. He reversed into a post and the car got a dent then he was angry at mommy for not telling him that the post was there.

I like to tease mommy's hair and put rollers and give her fancy hairstyles. I cut Bena's hair too but one day she was really angry at me. She had to go to school with scotch tape on her forehead because I cut her linzee too short. I think when I grow up I will be a hairdresser but daddy said I can't be a hairdresser. I have to do something better than that. I love the feel of hair and I am happy when I can do things with it. I can't draw or paint but when I plait or tease hair, it makes me feel really good.

Diary, do you remember that time when mommy was in the hospital to get her appendix out? Auntie Betty took me to see her at St Josephs. I wanted to look special for her so I teased my hair and made a very tall beehive on my head. There was so much hair to tease. That was not a good idea to tease hair that was all the way to my bottom into a beehive. It made me look like a Mother Sally on stilts. I was so proud of myself though, I did it all by myself even though I had a million clips in my hair. Auntie Betty looked at me before we went but she didn't say anything. I think she wanted to laugh. I was so excited to go to the hospital to see mommy because I didn't see her for a few days and she could see how I made my own beehive. She took one look at me and started to laugh and told Auntie Betty to take me out of the room before her stitches break. Auntie Betty said that I did a good job and mommy was happy to see me but I wish mommy would have said that. I don't know how many

hours I spent combing out the knots from my hair that night.
I wanted to take the scissors and cut it off but I would get into
trouble. I didn't talk to you that night or many nights after that
because my hands were tired from all that combing and pulling.
I think I only have half of my hair on my head now because I
pulled out so much.

Dear diary,

Diary the riots last year were bad. Lots of East Indian women
got killed and raped. When I asked mommy what rape means,
she said that I am too young to know. I looked it up in the dictionary but I didn't ask any more questions because mommy
didn't want to talk. I know it's bad but I don't know how bad.
Diary, life is so serious these days. When I was little I wanted
to grow up and then I would be able to talk all I want but now
I think growing up is not so easy. Soon I'll have to go to a new
school and leave my friends at Belair School. I don't want life
to change anymore but I don't know how to stop it. Daddy
doesn't let us go out after dark because he thinks bad things will
happen to us. He says a girl child has to be careful. So he takes
us everywhere with him and mommy has to drive us where ever
we go. He even thinks I have to dress different and not be such
a tomboy because I'm getting tall and I have to take an interest in myself. After all, people judge girls different from boys.
Sometimes I wonder if boys have it easier but then I think boys
are not allowed to do lots of things that girls have to do but then
again, boys get to do lots of things that girls will never get to do.
Maybe when I grow up life will be different. Maybe girls will
take care of boys and boys will take care of girls and everybody
will be happy.

Dear Diary,

Now that I am ten I spend so much time studying for my
Common Entrance examination and plucking chickens that I

hardly have time to write to you. If I don't pass, I have so stay at Belair school with the other children. I really don't mind though because I'm already in Form 1 and I should really only be in Standard 4 for my age. If I pass common entrance, I have to go to another school but they won't put me in Form 2 because all the children have to start in Form 1 when they pass the examination. So that means that I have to do form 1 over again like a proper dunce. That makes me feel shame but mommy said that I'm only supposed to be in Standard 4 but because I started school early, I am in one class advanced. It still makes me ashamed but Devika and Nandani and Janet will all have to start at Form 1 like me and they are bright so I shouldn't feel like a dunce.

The riots stopped now but everybody is scared. People don't want to go to Georgetown because of all the choke and rob men. Daddy is still working at the milk plant so he has to go to town and mommy is running the chicken business so she doesn't have to go to town. She stopped working at Kawall when she started minding chickens so Neighbour doesn't have to take care of us too much.

Dear diary,

Today was not a good day for me. Daddy scolded me when I got home. He said that I was rude to Grandfather Kartoon because I didn't say good morning to him on my way to school. I don't even remember that. I had to go to his house and say that I am sorry and it will never happen again. I didn't do it on purpose. Every morning when I go to school, I have to say good morning to all the relatives so before I even leave our yard I start with Good Morning Auntie Betty or Uncle Ramdat. They live next door. Then I have to say Good Morning grandfather Kaaza. He lives next door to auntie Betty. As soon as I meet the corner to turn to go to school, I have to say Good Morning Grandfather Charlie, Good Morning Grandfather Doobraj, Good Morning

Grandfather Subraj, Good Morning Grandfather Walter. They live on the left hand side of the road next to each other. Then I have to turn my head to the right and say Good morning Grandfather Kartoon, Good morning Grandfather Indar. They live on the right hand side next to each other. Then I have to turn my head quickly to the left again and say Good Morning Grandfather John, Good morning Grandfather Prem, Good Morning Grandfather Gunu. They live next to each other. Then quickly to the right again and if Grandfather Sensee is standing by the dam, I have to say good morning to him too. Then I have to turn quickly to the left again and say good morning grandfather Toi, Then I walk for a few houses and say good morning Grandmother Bhan and one last turn to the right to say good morning Grandfather Bap or Uncle Boysee, and if Mr Haynes is at his gate, I have to say good morning to him too. Then I can turn into the school yard. That's a lot of grandfathers each day and I have to do it again when I go home from school at lunch. Then I have to do it when I go back to school at lunch. Only this time I have to say good afternoon. Then I have to do it when I go home from school in the afternoon.

That's four times every day diary so you can see how I could miss one or two grandfathers. That's not even counting the uncles and aunties if they are in their yard sweeping or looking over their fences. And sometimes I have to shout because if I pretend I don't see them, they will call out my name after I pass their house and say that they are going to tell my parents that I am being rude. By the time I get to school I have to do the same thing with my teachers and the headmaster. No wonder I can't remember how to do my sums sometimes.

What I don't understand diary is how come I have so many grandfathers when most people only have two. After I said sorry to Grandfather Kartoon, I came home and asked Daddy. He said that they not actually my grandfathers but they are family so I have to call them grandfather. I said I only have one real grandfather and Nana is the one. Daddy said that it is a sign of respect and Indian people do that. I mean diary, how was I supposed to know that? Grandfather Kartoon should not have told Daddy. I always wonder how come they don't have anything to do but sit on their veranda all day and wait for the children to do something bad like not say good morning and they rush out to complain so we can get into trouble. Maybe that's their job to make children get into trouble. Nana is not like that though. He waits for me to come to his house and he smiles and is happy to see me each week. I love him a lot. I like the other grandfathers but mostly I am scared that they will get me in trouble so I say good morning or good afternoon. One day I should pretend that I am blind like Salim and then they will have to say good morning to me. Only thing is that I will have to do it for a long time. Maybe I shouldn't do that because I might get blind.

1965

Dear dairy,

Today we had a jandi and I always like it because I get to see lots of relatives especially the ones who live at Dekendren. The only thing I don't like is how long it takes. The pandit talks in Hindi so I get bored because I don't understand. The other children say some of the prayers but I don't think they know what the prayers mean. I asked the pandit after and he said that my daddy should send me to hindi lessons. I don't think he knows what the prayers mean either. He was just telling me that so I would stop asking. Some pandits are not nice. They act like they are smarter than us but I think they are just pretending. I don't like to touch their feet so I make sure that I stand far from them when I go to a jandi. Something inside of me makes me not want to do that but I don't know what that is. Only some people can be pandits and no girls can ever be a pandit. I asked daddy why we have to touch the pandit's foot and he said that they are like god. They are not like god. God has clean feet and nice toe nails not ugly ones like some of the pandits. They should cut their toenails and scrub their foot so it's clean and soft like mommy's foot. Mommy said that Muslims don't have to touch the mai-jee's feet. I think I will just be a muslim and a christian and stop being a hindu. I don't know if I can do that. Since daddy is a hindu, then I will have a stay a hindu. Since mommy is a muslim, then I will have to be a muslim too. And since me and Bena and Karran are baptized at the Lutheran church, I will still have to be a Christian too. Maybe that is a good thing. Maybe I can pick the things I like and not do the things I don't like. I don't like to touch the pandit's feet so I won't do that. And I really don't like when I have to go to Nani's house for Koranshareef and they do circumcisions for the boys at the orphanage. The boys scream sometimes when they are doing it and I want to run away but I have to stay. This is one very good time dairy that I am very glad to be a girl.

Diary, I am glad that I don't have to spell perfect for you. I am sure some of these words are spelled wrong. When I grow up and I do Koranshareefs, I won't include circumcisions for boys. So far I like being a christian but I don't like when the pastor at Redeemer church say that we are all sinners. I try to be a good person but he says we are all born from sin. I thought we were born from love. I asked mommy why he would say that but she says that it is in the bible. Sometimes when he is at the front, he shouts and I get scared that he is angry with me but it's the way he talks. It's like those people in the big tents at the revival meetings. Lots of negroes are in the tents and they clap and sing very loud. I never went but I hear them sometimes and neighbour says that they perform miracles and make cripple people walk again.

Dear diary,

A good thing happened yesterday. It is almost the end of August and I thought I had to go to back to Belair school because I didn't pass the common entrance exam. Grandfather Baba promised that he would buy me a bicycle if I passed. He said that I would get the bicycle because I am smart but my name was not in the newspaper so that means that I did not pass. All my friends are going to secondary school because they passed.

Daddy was angry and said I skylark too much and I should have studied harder but I studied as hard as I could. Grandfather Baba told daddy to check to see if the newspaper made a mistake but daddy said no the paper does not make mistakes so I must have failed. He said he wasted a lot of money on extra lessons and I still failed. Grandfather said to go down to the ministry of education and check the results because he knows that I am smart enough to pass. You know what diary? The newspaper made a mistake. I passed and I got placed at Cummings Lodge Government Secondary School. Mommy had to hurry to go to Fogarty's to get the orange uniform cloth and a tie for that school and daddy got the booklist to buy my books. Good thing Grandfather made daddy go or I would have missed my scholarship and still be at Belair school or daddy would have to send me to another school and pay lots of school fees. Sometimes newspapers make mistakes but this one could have changed my life because I would not have got my bicycle and daddy would punish me and make me work harder at Belair school and I would have to hear how I was a dunce every day.

Dear Diary,

I love it at Cumming's Lodge school. I have lots of friends and I like to play cricket and volleyball with the boys. Lots of the girls want to keep the pleats in their uniforms nice and creased but I don't care. My pleats are not very nice. I mean diary that I start out each day with clean socks and shoes and my uniform looks nice but I cannot keep it that way if I play sports. I play rounders and can hit the ball very far so the older girls let me bat a lot and I can catch good too. I ride my bike every day and park it next to the front steps by the prefects and teachers door. We are not allowed to use those steps. Only the prefects and teachers can use it. We have to walk all the way around the school even though my class is right next to the steps. Sometimes when no one is looking, I walk there anyway. I don't know why we cannot use the steps. It is a stupid rule. If they catch me, I will get detention.

I am in Form 1A. That's for the smart students. Then Form 1B is for the next smartest. Then 1C is for the not so smart students. We were all smart enough to pass Common Entrance to get into the school so why should we be divided into smart and dunce? I am just glad that I am in 1A though. Some teachers are not nice at all. They treat the students in 1C as if they are stupid and call them names. I like that Nandani and Janet came from Belair school to Cumming's Lodge so at least I had some friends who I know but it didn't take me long to make lots of new friends.

Dear diary,

Something funny happened at school last week but I didn't have time to tell you. Amna and I sit in the same bench. I was talking to her and not listening to the teacher so I had to move and sit beside Manikchand Sookram. The teacher put me to sit beside him so I won't talk but I just kept talking to him. He is so quiet that he doesn't say anything at all. I make him talk to me because I just keep asking him till he answers. He is so shy that he won't take his lunch container out of his school bag. He sticks his head in the bag and puts the food in his mouth then lifts up his head and chews. Today I reached into his school bag and took out his lunch kit and put it on the desk because I wanted to see what he was eating. I told him that when he doesn't want to eat his lunch and wants to go instead to Auntie Eunice's shop to buy his lunch, I will take it and share it with the other girls so he doesn't throw it out or take it home and get into trouble with his mom for not eating. We save some of our food for after school when the girls are waiting for the train. That's a good plan but sometimes the food spoils before we can eat it because it is cooked early in the morning and the heat all day makes it spoil. We should have a fridge in the school but then again, not too many people have a fridge. My friends say that I am rich because we have a fridge. They always say that but I don't think that I am rich. I just have some things that they don't have.

Dear dairy,

Today Jerome Khan got into trouble from Mr. Kamar. He is a very strict head master. He was standing at the upstairs corridor today and he was peeping into our classroom. He does that a lot. He sneaks up on us as if he is always looking for us to do something bad. Jerome sits behind me and he was untying my ribbon from the end of my plait and tying it to the back of the bench so that when I get up, the bench will pull my hair. Because my hair is very long, he could do that without me knowing. Mr. Kamar saw him doing it and came downstairs and caned him in front of the whole class. I felt bad because Jerome was only playing. I know my hair would have hurt but I didn't want him to be caned for a silly thing like that. At least Jerome didn't have to get a caning in front of the whole school.

Mr. Kamar uses the wild cane a lot during school assembly when he flogs the boys and girls who misbehave. The boys have to bend over a table and they get four lashes across their bottom. The girls have to stretch out their hands and get four lashes. Sometimes he canes them so hard that their hands bleed from the hitting. It's horrible diary, just horrible. Because I am in Form 1A and my last name starts with B, I have to stand in the front row right next to the stage where Mr. Kamar is standing at the pulpit. That's not the right name but I am so upset that I can't think of the right name. When he goes over to the table where he is doing the caning, I can see how hard he is doing it and it looks very awful. I can see a look in his eyes as if he likes to do it, as if he wants to make them cry. Sometimes I can see that the boys want to cry because it hurts so much but they try to act brave. It is so stupid to beat your students. If I ever become a teacher, I will never do that to my students.

1966

Dear diary,

I am really upset. Daddy gave my bicycle to Bena to go to school because she can't get to her school by train. That's my bike that I got from Grandfather Baba as a gift. Daddy should buy her one of her own. I am not happy about that. I have to take the train to school now but I don't mind. Paul saves a seat for me every day. I hail off the train like he does so I don't have as far to walk. It is not safe because sometimes the train is moving fast and when I jump off the train, the gravel makes me skid but each day I am getting better. None of the girls do it, only boys. Daddy saw some boys hailing off the train and I think he knows that I will want to try so he warned me never to do that because if I fall on the gravel when I jump off, the train can suck me under so I don't hail off at Belair only at Industry.

Last week the five of us were waiting for the train after school – me, Orleen, Beatrice, Nandani and Gail. We were sharing our leftover food from lunch and Orleen had some good dumplings so I asked if I could have one. The other girls looked at me and I know they were thinking that I shouldn't eat from her because she is black but her dumplings looked good so I ate one. They told me after that I was nasty to eat from Orleen. When I asked why, they said that black people can eat from Indians but it was not good for Indians to eat from Negroes because they are not clean. I went home and told mommy and she said that I eat from Neighbour so I can eat from other black people. My friends said that Neighbour is my servant so she can cook food for me at my house but I am not supposed to go to her house and eat food. That is really stupid. Neighbour lives downstairs of us so our house is her house and besides when mommy goes to work and we don't like what she cooks, we go to Neighbour's kitchen and eat her food. She makes smoke herrings with pepper. Mommy doesn't let her cook that upstairs because she doesn't like the smell or taste so we just go to neighbour's house and eat it but we don't tell mommy. I think Orleen was happy that I ate her dumpling because she offers me food each day now. The other girls have started eating her food too and we don't even care about Negro and Indian anymore.

Dear diary,

British Guiana got independence so we are now Guyana. I will have to get used to saying Guyana not BG. Uncle Boysee is very happy that the British is not in charge anymore. He said that the CIA helped Forbes Burnham to win the election and they even paid for the riots and looting. I don't know who the CIA is but I didn't ask anything about that. At least the riots are done and it is safe now. Cheddi is not happy but at least he is not in jail. Every year we will celebrate May 26th as our independence. I think some of the islands are getting their independence too but I don't know which one. We don't have to worry about soldiers and guns but Daddy said we have to worry now about how we are going to live. I hope he can get a job closer to home. When he has to go to McKenzie, we are all alone in the house and I think that thieves will come and thief or hurt us. They are plentiful these days and daddy said that they are desperate. They mostly steal fowls and ducks but I am afraid that they will break into the house. Mommy said that Flossie is the best guard dog in the world but thieves are poisoning dogs so they may poison Flossie too. She is a good protector and doesn't eat from anyone except us so maybe she'll be safe.

Last week at night daddy was home and we heard some sounds in the back yard like coconuts falling from the tree. When he went out to check, he saw a whole thrush of coconuts so he knew someone was in the tree but when he called out, no one answered. Daddy can get crazy sometimes. He called a few times and still no one answered. He called Karran to bring a cutlass and said he would chop down the coconut tree. It was at least forty or fifty feet tall so whoever was in the tree would either have to come down or fall down when the tree was chopped down. Daddy made two chops at the bottom and I couldn't believe my eyes diary. Somebody started sliding down slowly and then stopped. Daddy chopped one more time and the person came all the way down. It was our neighbour Benjee. Daddy usually pays him to climb the very tall coconut trees to get the young coconut. He is a good climber. He ties a cloth or rope around his ankle and quick time he is up the tree. I tried to do that but I can't hold on so after a few feet, I have to come down. I didn't think he would steal from us though. The other children say that he is a thief and he uses the money to buy cigarettes but I never saw him thiefing anything. Mother Bear is going to be sad that her son is thiefing the neighbour's coconut. Daddy went up to him with the cutlass and put it on his neck while he was shining the torchlight in Benjee's face and said "If you ever put foot in this yard again, I will use this cutlass. You hear me boy?" Benjee walked home and we saw someone else run out of some bushes and run away but because it was dark, we couldn't see who it was. There was more than one of them. Maybe Benjee thought daddy went back to McKenzie so he wanted to thief. That's why I want daddy to come home.

1967

Dear diary,

Daddy is working at McKenzie now and we don't see him that much. That's not a bad thing though. We can play a bit more and do more skylarking in the afternoons. I miss Devika because we are going to different schools but I talk to her almost every afternoon. She got to go to Bishops High where the really smart students go but I like Cumming's Lodge. I don't like the orange colour of my uniforms. She gets to wear a nice green one. People know from the colour of our uniforms and ties which school we go to and I can see that some of the students think they are better than us because they wear a uniform from a different school. Cumming's Lodge is not for the students with the highest marks. It's midway. The schools in town have students with higher marks like Saints, Bishops, Queens and Tutorial High.

Daddy comes home only on the weekends because McKenzie is far away and he can only get there by a speed boat. The government is building a highway to connect Georgetown to McKenzie so maybe he will come home more. It is quiet around the house at night and sometimes I don't feel safe but the riots are over and it is mostly peaceful.

Daddy and Mommy bought a house lot in Chateau Margot where the old dutch chimney is. They are going to build a concrete house there. Daddy showed us the floor plan and it will have an inside toilet and bathroom and a nice big kitchen and there will be louver windows all around. Bena and I will still have our own room but it will have only one door which can close and people don't have to walk through to go to the living room like we have now. I think it's going to be so nice to live in a fancy house. We can finally leave the old house in Belair but I don't know if I want to live so far away from my family. I wish it was here in Belair instead of so far away. We will have no family there but mommy said that we can drive to Belair whenever we want to visit. Right now I can sit on the front steps and see everyone who is passing by but if we go to Chateau, we won't be able to see anyone because it's not even near the public road.

Diary do you remember the time we went to Chateau with the school to visit the chimney? I forgot to tell you about that. We learned about how the dutch lived in Guyana and how they gave the whole country to the British a long time ago. They must be really rich to do that. They gave the land and all the people but I didn't think you could give away people. We learned about how British Guiana had a lot of slaves and how the British used to buy and sell people and how the slaves used to be treated badly. That's terrible. I don't know if the dutch used to own slaves. I used to find some pieces of broken blue and white plates and clay jugs and blue in the backyard when we used to dig up the backyard to bury the feathers and sawdust from the chicken coops. Maybe the dutch lived in our yard before I lived here.

Some of the old people in Belair say that they are glad England is not ruling us anymore because they did some bad things to a lot of negro and indian people. They brought many negroes from Africa to be slaves and when they couldn't do that anymore, they tricked many Indians to come to Guyana and promised them that they would be given lots of money if they planted the cane fields but the British people never paid the money so many poor Indians who came from India had to stay in Guyana because they had no money to go back to India. Daddy said that sometimes his grandfather Sanichar would cry when he was talking because he was so sad. Sanichar would tell him how the British gave a lot of swamp land to the Indians instead of money that they owed because the land was no good for planting cane and would get flooded a lot. The indian people knew how to plant rice so most of them were getting rich because they know how to flood and drain the land to grow rice.

Daddy said that his father Ramsahoye owned a lot of land in Belair when he was young but he had to sell a lot of it to send his brothers to school. I am glad daddy doesn't have to sell his home to send me to school because I got a scholarship.

Dear diary,

The house at Chateau is starting to look nice. Mommy goes there every day to see how the workmen are doing and she is not happy sometimes. She said that they are thiefing some of the lumber so she has to go and spend almost all day there. She had to hire a watchman at night so that people don't come and thief the lumber and concrete mix. Diary, I like the new green Toyota Carona that mommy is driving. We have two cars now. Daddy did some work for Mr. Millington at McKenzie and he could not pay daddy so he gave daddy the car instead. Mommy picks me up from school every afternoon when she is going home from Chateau. I bring Janet and June with me to the public road and give them a drop to Liliendaal because mommy has to pass there before we get home. I asked Nandani but she wants to take the train with the other girls so she doesn't come. Sometimes mommy comes right to the school and my friends think that my parents have a lot of money because we are building a new house and we have two cars. I don't really think about it but I am glad that I can go home early sometimes. I miss being at the train station with my friends though.

Dear diary,

I wish I was doing better in school. I feel stupid sometimes because I don't always understand the Mathematics and Physics classes. More and more I can see that the teachers only favour the students who are good at those subjects especially Mr. Perceval. Everyone says that he is very smart but when I go to his class, I don't understand most of it. I really like Mr. Johnson's English and literature classes. I read a lot and I like the books he tells us to read. I think he is really smart and I am doing good in his classes. I am in 3A now but I think if I don't do better this year, I'll be in 4B next year.

I like to play rounders and cricket but if I play cricket, I have to play with the boys because we don't have a girls team. I am good at volleyball too. I am in B House and the teachers want me to do sprinting in track and field but I don't like to run and I am not very good at it. I am very good at long jump, high jump, discus and javelin but no good at running. I think because I am tall, the teachers think I should be good at that but I really hate it. June Grannum is in E House and she is a fast runner. No one can beat her and even if I come in second, she is way ahead of me. Everyone says that Negroes can run very fast so Indians should use their brains because they can't run as fast. Well June is Negro and she can run fast but there are some Indian boys that can run very fast too. Our school doesn't have a lot of black students so maybe that's why the Indians have a chance.

At least nowadays we don't talk so much about Indians and negroes but we just know that we are not like them. No one talks about it but we all know. Errol Benn and June and Orleen are black but I don't see how they are different. We still share our lunches with each other – well Errol goes home for lunch. Some of the students say that I am a town girl so that's why I don't think like country people. Country people have more bad experiences with black people than town people. I explain that I am not a town person, that I live in Belair which is not really Georgetown but they say that Belair is for rich people so black people can't afford to live there. I tell them that Mr. Powley, Mr. Haynes, Mr. Commerbadge, Mrs. Kanes and Jennifer Jones and her family live in Belair live but they say that if I can count all the black people who live there, then I am proving them right. I know I was trying to outsmart them by calling out all the black families but Mr. Cummerbadge lives in Gutter Dam with lots of other black people and Mrs. Kanes and Doreen and Alington live in Blygiezeit. Those places are not really part of Belair but Mr. Cummbadge comes next door to shop at Auntie Betty's shop and Mrs. Kanes is a servant for Devika so I count them.

I should really count Lucille too because she is our servant but she is a fair skin black. They say that her father is white but he doesn't want her and her mother because her mother was his servant and she got a baby for him. Pecky is like that too. He is fair skinned and has brassy coloured steel wool hair but he lives in Gutter Dam too so I really can't count him. Sometimes I used to feel sorry for him when he got licks from the teachers at Belair School but he really is dunce. The teachers call him worthless so he says that he is not going to try at school. One day he was teasing me at the front yard and daddy heard him and yelled at him so since that time, he walks by the yard but doesn't look in if he sees daddy.

There are a lot of black people who are servants in Belair but they don't live in Belair. I don't really know where they live. They just come to people's yard and ask for work and people hire them. Auntie Betty hired Roddy to work for her and he is very strong. He lifts a 200 pound bag of copra as if it is so easy. He lives at their house in the downstairs part. People say that black people are dirty but Roddy bathes every morning and afternoon and he powders up himself so much that sometimes he looks white. He always smells like baby powder and he takes care of us if he sees anybody trying to bother us. He works from Monday to Saturday from early morning to late at night and he goes home on Sunday to Bachelor's Adventure to visit his family. I asked him if he has any children but he just smiles and says yes but they never come to visit him at Belair. I wonder if he misses them.

I miss daddy when he is away at McKenzie. We went there one time in the Toyota Carona to visit him because the new highway is opened. The Millingtons live in a very big house and they cooked lots of food. McKenzie is very red and dusty and

I've never seen a place like that. It's the bauxite that they mine there. I am not sure what kind of work daddy does there. I think he works in the office. I wouldn't want to live there because it is very far away from Georgetown and there are a lot of black people living nearby in Wismar so I am kind of scared since the riots but Daddy said that if you are good to people, they will be good to you. When the riots were taking place a few years ago, a lot of Indian women were raped and one woman had a broken bottle inserted into her private parts. The newspaper said that she died from bleeding. Those were terrible years but now that we have our independence, things are quieter but Indians still don't go to Wismar and only a few of them live in McKenzie. Mr. Millington is partly black so he is safe but daddy is Indian. Maybe if he stays close to his workplace, he should be safe.

Dear Diary,

The house at Chateau Margot is finally finished and it is so beautiful. You should see the kitchen. I already planned to practice my baking in the new kitchen especially when mommy is not at home. There is a nice bathroom with tiles on the inside and a flush toilet. Now I know what my friends are saying that I am lucky. None of them have a house like this. The louver windows are sparkling. The floors are shiny greenheart wood and the walls are solid concrete. I already planned to invite my friends for parties every week but now that it is done, I have a different feeling. I like the house but I don't like that it's so far away from all my family and friends. The house has been locked up for a few weeks already because me and Bena and Karran don't want to leave Belair. I know we should move into it but I like this old house right here in Belair even though the roof leaks most times when it rains. Dad said that's when duck has water to bathe and fowl is glad for some to drink. He has one of those sayings for every occasion. Auntie Betty said we should not have let daddy waste all that money on a new house and then we wouldn't go and live in it. She doesn't understand. I don't want to leave all my friends and family in Belair and go all the way to Chateau Margot.

Auntie Betty was just saying that because she was angry with me but she is right. I have to tell you the reason she was angry. I went next door to her shop with the shop book and I bought some tinned sausages, continental biscuits and a bottle of cider for me and Bena and Karran to have a little party while mommy was out. Daddy told her that whenever we go over to her shop with the shop book, she has to give us whatever we want and write it down in the book and when he comes home every weekend from McKenzie, he will pay her. Sometimes she thinks that we buy things that we don't need just because daddy can pay for it so she got angry and told us about moving to Chateau. That week and the next week, we didn't buy a single thing while daddy was away and when he looked through the shop book he asked me why we didn't buy anything for two weeks. I said we didn't need anything because we are getting too big for silly parties with just the three of us. He didn't believe me because I am not good at telling lies. My face still turns red when I try to do that so he knows that I am lying. He asked me to tell him why I didn't buy anything so I told him that Auntie Betty was angry and told us that we are ungrateful. He went over to her shop and yelled at her and told her never to tell his children that they are ungrateful. She has to give us whatever we want and he will pay for it. I really didn't buy sweets and biscuits after that because she was right. Even though that was an awful thing to say to us, we would miss her because we lived in Belair since I was a baby so this is my home even if it's an old house.

1968

Dear diary,

Daddy sold all his chickens and bought a truck to start a trucking business. He said that since he made a lot of money from his chicken business, everyone wants to do it but they keep their chicken coops dirty so the whole place smells terrible when it rains and the chicken litter gets wet. Raymond and Ali were burning dead chickens because they all got a disease. Daddy told them that they have to keep the coops clean but because so many people are raising chickens, diseases spread from one fowl pen to the others in Belair and now there are lots of dead chickens when the feathers burn, it smells terrible. I am glad daddy isn't raising chickens anymore. I am glad we don't have to stay up late to pluck the chickens because I get so tired in school the next day that I can't concentrate. Mommy said that it was too much work for children to be doing.

Daddy gets lots of orders for sand already so he is really busy. A lot of people are building concrete houses now so he goes to the sandpit by 4am and gets a load of sand. By the time my train comes at 7:30, he is coming home for breakfast after delivering his first load of sand. Every morning he stops to ask if I have money to go to school with and sometimes I say yes and sometimes no. My friends think that I should say no every time even if I have money so I can get more. I get 50 cents a week but if I use it up I can always ask him for more. They think I am lucky that I can get as much money as I want. Some weeks I don't even have anything to buy with my money. Other weeks I run out and if Daddy asks, I tell him I don't have any and he gives me more. Daddy likes me to wear clean uniform and socks every day and he stops at the train line to check. Salim passes sometimes with his basket on his head. He knows my voice when I tell him good morning and he still calls me his angel even though I am now going to high school and I don't help him sell anymore. I still feel so sorry for him. He works very hard to take care of his family but as a blind man, someone should be taking care of him. Sometimes I talk about this when I am waiting for the train but it doesn't seem to bother my friends as much as it bothers me that he is blind and no one helps him.

Dear Diary,

School started this week and I am now in Form 4A. I was so glad to see my friends. I must have grown a lot because all the girls are a lot shorter than me. We got a new mathematics teacher. His name is Mr. Ferguson and he is from Canada in a place named Winnipeg. He's very tall and has blonde hair and he sweats a lot even when he is standing in the shade on the corridor. He looks like he's been running for a long time because his face is very red. When he started on Monday, Mr. Mohan Singh and Mr. Taharally had a lot of the older boys picketing outside of school. They had signs saying yankee go home and they said that the white teachers were taking jobs from Guyanese teachers. I was watching from the stage and Mr. Ferguson looked a bit scared when they walked up to him and waved the pickets at him. They are not nice to him so I feel sorry for him. Monday was his first day and when he came in to class, we stood up and said "Good Morning Sir." He looked surprised so he said good morning and walked very quickly to the front and sat in his chair as if he didn't know what else to do. After a couple minutes, I told him that he had to tell us to sit down because we are not allowed to sit until the teacher tells us. We have to do whatever the teachers tell us to do or Mr. Kamar will cane us. We're not supposed to ask any questions or they call us obstreperous and insipid. Mr. Johnson told me last year to learn a new word every day from the dictionary and at the end of each year, I will know 365 new words. When I heard Mr. Singh use those words to me last year outside the staff room,

I looked them up in the dictionary. Those are cruel words but teachers get to talk to us like that and we can't say anything because they punish us. Mr. Singh is especially rude to us and he hits too and the reason he called me those names was because I told him that the girls toilet was running over with water and the taps were not working.

I remember one day when one of the boys threw a water balloon on Mr. Aregi's head from the second floor and when I wouldn't say who it was, we all got a caning. The headmaster knew that I saw who it was but wouldn't say so he was angry at all of us. When I went home I was scared to show my hands to daddy because I thought I would get another caning but he was angry that the teacher hit me so hard that I couldn't hold my fork at dinner. I had blisters on both hands and my right hand was cut and bleeding from the caning. Daddy drove me to school the next day and went to the headmaster's office. When Mr. Kamar called the teacher to the office, Daddy grabbed him by his collar and told him that if he ever hit me like that again, daddy would take me to the police and lay charges. I never got a caning at school again but some of the other students get a caning almost every week. I don't know why some of the teachers hit like that. And none of the parents complain so the teachers just keep doing it. We are told that we have to show respect for our teachers but some of them don't treat us very nice so they don't deserve any respect.

Dear diary,

I like talking to Mr. Ferguson. He makes us take notes in Mathematics classes. He is the first teacher who ever made us take notes in Mathematics. Usually the teachers in the other classes spend most of the class writing notes on the chalkboard and we spend most of our time copying them and many times when we don't understand, we are not allowed to ask any questions. The other mathematics teachers are worse. They tell us the equations and we can write them in our notebooks but most of the time I write the formulae but don't know what they mean and I don't know when to use them. I feel that I am going to fail mathematics this year. I usually do well in English and literature, but the other subjects are hard and the teachers are not helpful. They have their favourites and if you are not good in their subject, you are not a favourite.

Well I am not a favourite of several teachers but I do like Mr. Ferguson and I am getting better in Mathematics because he is making it easier to understand algebra, geometry, trig and logarithms. He explains the equations and formulae but more carefully than the other teachers who make us memorize them and then I never know which one to use to solve a problem because they never make sense. I think that's why I only got 6 out of 100 on my Physics test. I'm really not good in Physics. Mr. Persaud talks into his chest and doesn't explain anything, especially to girls. We light the bunsen burners to do some experiments but he never comes to check to see if mine is good. He is one of those teachers who have their favourites and I am not one. Maybe it's because I talk too much.

Mr. Johnson is really good though. I love going to his English and Literature classes and he said that I am an excellent student. I do fine in Chemistry and now I am doing better in Mathematics but I prefer English and Literature and Spanish sometimes. Diary, do you remember the time I got 3 out of 100 in Latin? That was bad but at least I got some marks. A few people got naught. That chemistry set that Uncle Merican bought for me is fun but we don't do those kinds of experiments in class. Actually, we don't do any experiments in class. I remember when he came from England and he stayed with us. He smelled like Yardley's powder and he ate peppermint gum. He said I was very smart and he wanted to buy me a gift. He said that I could ask for anything so I asked for a chemistry set. I still remember him laughing and he looked just like daddy. He thought I would ask for a dress or shoes, not a chemistry set.

I ask Mr. Ferguson so many questions about Canada. He tells me about the different seasons, hockey and baseball and salted popcorn and root beer and putting sugar on his grapefruit instead of salt. He said there is this restaurant in Winnipeg called A and W where you can drive up in your car and order food and they will bring it out to you on a tray and you eat it in your car. I think that's how all white people live in Canada. They stay in their car like Mr. Jury and people bring out the food to them. Mr. Ferguson said that I am very curious about everything but he doesn't mind when I ask him things about Canada. I wonder how people live there? I think of it like a Christmas card with carriages in the snow and everyone is happy and has lots of money I think they also have a lot of dead trees because the snow kills them.

He said winter is very cold and he is longing for a glass of root beer and some of the food that he is used to eating. Salt on popcorn doesn't sound as good as sugar. I went home one day when we were talking about how cold Canada is and I had a great idea. I made Karran stand outside of the big freezer that we keep plucked chickens in before Daddy used to take them to the supermarket and I climbed in and made him shut the door. I only stayed in for a minute because it was very cold. I don't think I would want to live in Canada. I don't really understand how people don't die from the cold. I told Mr. Ferguson what I did and he said that Canadians wear fur coats and gloves and hats in the winter. It's like that Dr. Chivago movie daddy took us to see. I didn't understand a thing about the movie but there was so much snow and the man's mouth was frozen. I am really glad I live in Guyana where it is sunny. Well, there is flooding in the rainy season and a lot of mosquitoes but I still like living here.

Dear diary,

I forgot to mention that Mr. Ferguson gave me lines to write because I was throwing chalk at him. I thought it was a funny thing to do when his head was turned toward the blackboard but he didn't think so. It was a long sentence and I had to write it 70 times. I begged and begged and he said he would reduce it to 69 times. This is what I had to write "Hurling chalky projectiles at mathematics teachers is a malicious act and such social malignancy must be stopped before chaos rules supreme." Who ever heard of writing three or four lines 70 times? Well I learned lots of new words but I wish I didn't have to learn them that way. I still like him but he still sweats a lot even when he is only watching us play cricket at lunch. He just stands there at the railings and sweats. He is the first white person that I have really talked to and he is nice. I think the other teachers don't like it that I talk to him but he answers all my questions without being cross about it.

Lots of white people live in Guyana but they treat most of us like we are their servants and they don't have Indian or black friends. Lots of them live in Belair Gardens but there is a gate at the entrance and a guard sits there and guards their houses. We can't go into the compound. The only Indian or black people who go there are servants and they have to leave at the end of the day. The guard treats us like thieves even though he is Indian too. He acts like he owns one of the houses but he only gets to sit in a little hut at the gate so I don't know why he acts like that. Sometimes I want to throw a rock at the windows of some of the houses but I will get into trouble.

I feel awful when I think back of the time when I was still in primary school and I visited Uncle Gun's house. He lives in Belair Park where a lot of white people live because he came back from England and he is teaching at the Technical Institute. I did a really awful thing that day. Angela and Sharon said that white people are not always nice and we don't have to be nice to them so when I was swinging really high in one of their swings, the white children from next door came over to play and I threw plantain chips and fried channa on the ground and laughed when they ran and picked it up and ate it. Now that I talk to Mr. Ferguson, I think back to that day. I never did anything that terrible to people before and I don't even know why I did it. I could have come off the swing and give them some but I thought it was funny when Bena and Sharon and Angela started laughing but I knew in my mind that it was bad because if Daddy ever saw me doing that, he would flog me especially because every Sunday when we were eating breakfast, he would invite beggars who were passing by to eat with us. Diary, why would I do such an awful thing to the children when they were not bad? My face is turning red now that I am writing it because I am still embarrassed.

1969

Dear diary,

Daddy is getting lots of contracts for sand from people especially from the government department of Housing. I know that because I have to type up all the invoices and I have to say I hate typing. I am taking typing in school and also sewing but it's really embroidery so it isn't very useful and we type the same things over and over asdf ;lkj asdf ;lkj asdf ;lkj. I can't seem to keep my hand on the right keys without looking. The boys get to do technical drawing and woodwork and the girls have to do sewing and typing. I would like to do woodworking but one of the teachers said it was because I want to be with the boys. They don't understand that I don't want to type and I don't see how embroidering pillowcases will be very useful when I grow up. It's not like I'll be able to sew a dress or shirt or even a pillowcase.

I know I do not want to be a typist so I'd better do well in school or I will be typing invoices for the rest of my life. I am not a very good typist and if I make a mistake on the invoice form, I have to start over again because the carbon paper gets all messy. I hate it. I almost want to go back to plucking chickens. Well I don't hate it that much but almost. I type up the invoices and Mommy goes to Housing to deliver it and get payment but sometimes it takes her all day to do that because the men there are not very helpful unless you bribe them.

Daddy says that he has to give a lot of bribes because when he goes to the sandpit, the people there will make you wait for a long time to get a load of sand unless you give them a small piece. Then when he goes on the East Bank road, the police will stop him for no good reason and if he doesn't give them some money, they will pull over his truck on some trumped up charges and make him wait. Then it's the same thing on the East Coast road if he has a load to deliver that way. Then when mommy goes to Housing, she has to give a bribe there too. Sometimes the foremen at Housing ask daddy to deliver a free load of sand to their house or to their family's house and he has to agree or else he doesn't get paid for a long time. So every day he loses almost one load for every five or six loads that he delivers.

I am so angry that he has to do that because he works very hard but he says that people are corrupt but it is the cost of doing business. I told him to go to the boss but he said that most times it's the boss man who wants the bribe so there is no one to tell. Everyone knows that it happens but no one talks about it. They just pay the bribes and go on with their business. Sometimes the lumber yards ask him to deliver lumber but he has to make two stops – one to the supervisor's home and one to the customer. He doesn't have to pay for the lumber because the supervisor steals it and loads it up on Daddy's truck but he has to use his time that he could be delivering another load. That is not right but no one wants to talk because their business will be affected. I thought independence would make us better for everyone but this is not better. Daddy says that sometimes it feels worse because the new foremen are worse than the white people who used to supervise them.

Dear diary,

It is now September and it is the beginning of my last year at Cumming's Lodge. Diary, I have been at this school for four years already and when I left in July, I was sad to leave because I would not see my friends for six weeks. This is the worst secret that I have to keep but I can tell you because you always listen and you're such a good friend. I am so afraid that if the head master finds out my secret, I will be expelled from school. Last month, this man came to Guyana from Canada and he was staying next door to us. He lives in Winnipeg. That's exactly the same place that Mr. Ferguson lives. That was a great surprise because now I know two people from Winnipeg. He is Kapil's cousin Robin and he is the photographer at Kapil's wedding. He was supposed to be looking for a wife because his parents told him that when he went to Guyana, he was supposed to look for a girl to marry. He spent a lot of time looking at a lot of girls but he couldn't find one that he liked. Many parents paraded their daughters in front of him and then he had to decide if that was the one he wanted to pick. It's like when people came to our house to buy chickens. They would go to the fowl pen and look over the chickens and when they find the one they want, they tell us catch it for them.

After two weeks of looking he didn't find anyone so Pappy – that's his uncle but we call him Pappy said that he should stop looking because there was a young girl just next door. They were talking about me! Robin said that I was too young but

Pappy said that was a good thing that I am only fifteen because Robin can mould me into the kind of woman he wants. Pappy came and asked daddy for me to marry Robin and daddy asked me. At first I thought it was a joke because I am only 15 and he is 22 so I laughed and said no. Daddy was not happy and he told me each time that I said no that I had to go back and think about it again. Daddy said that it was a good opportunity for me to go to Canada and I would have a good life but honestly diary, my life is good right now. I get everything I want. If I go to Canada, I will have to leave all my friends and family in Guyana and I will have to live with strangers. I finally said yes because I was tired after three days of saying no but I don't want to get married to a stranger. I want to stay in school.

The worse thing right now is that I am afraid that someone will find out that I am engaged to be married and then I will be expelled from school. I am so scared each night to go to sleep and every day that I wake up. I hope that no one will be spiteful and tell the headmaster. But I have good friends so they won't tell. I can't bear the thought of not seeing my friends every day and even though I am not the brightest student, I want to stay in school. Mommy said that since I was a little child, I wanted to go to school so I started nursery school at Grandfather Khartoon's bottom house when I was 2 years old because I used to stand on our front steps and cry when the older children were passing our house to go to school. I feel the same way now. I won't stop crying if I am expelled from school for getting engaged. I don't know any other student in our school who is engaged or married and is still in school.

Dear diary,

Today was the most horrible day in my life. When I came home, Mommy said that I received a letter from someone in Canada. Imagine my fright when I opened it and it was an anonymous letter in the mail from someone in Canada telling me that I should end my engagement to Robin. The person said that Robin doesn't love me and doesn't want to get married. I already know that because I don't love him or want to marry him either. The person said that I should write him and break off the engagement. I want to end it but my parents will not allow me to do that. The letter was very spiteful.

I really don't want to go to Canada. I have so many friends that I can hardly think of leaving all of them and I will miss Bena and Karran most of all. I am trying to think of how I can get out of this but there doesn't seem to be a way. I think of running away but I know that if I go to Auntie Bhano or Auntie Siloch, they will bring me back to Belair. I could go to Nani but daddy will go there and get me and he will be very angry at them for keeping me there. When he gets angry, everyone is afraid of him, especially us. I haven't been any other places without Mommy and Daddy so I don't even know where I would go. I have to come up with a plan but nothing is coming into my head. Diary, if you could talk, I am sure you'd tell me something.

.2.

ᵶ

1970

Dear diary,

It's been many months since I wrote to you. Well, it's almost time for me to finish school and then I leave for Canada on July 20ᵗʰ. So far Mr. Rambihar did not find out that I am engaged so I can write my O level exam. I am going to write five subjects but some people are writing 8. Do you remember that spiteful letter I got a few months ago? Well I got 4 more, each one more threatening than the last. The final one was last week and the person was threatening to kill me if I go to Canada. Four big words I WILL KILL YOU. They never sign their name. When mommy took the letter to show Pappy, he said that he suspected it was someone who knows Robin but he said that the person is a coward for writing anonymous letter to a child. Pappy thought I was old enough to get engaged and now I am a child. I feel like a child who is about to do something bad.

I really don't want to go to Canada but my parents will not listen. I told them that I am afraid that when I go, someone will kill me when I get off the plane, and I will have no one to protect me. I gave up trying to run away because none of my family would help me. They are all afraid of Daddy. Many girls have arranged marriages to people from Canada or England so my family wouldn't help me because they think that I am lucky to be going to Canada. Mommy and daddy got married because they loved each other and not because it was arranged so why would they do this to me? It was harder in 1952 when they got married especially when they were different religions. They said that at that time, Hindus and Muslims could be friends but they were not supposed get married. That's why they decided to baptize all of us in the Christian church. That way, none of the family would argue. But we all have Hindu and Christian names but not Muslim names.

Well, Mr. Ferguson is going to be there if I even get to Winnipeg. My Ferguson had to leave Cumming's Lodge before his time was up because his mom was ill so I finally told him that I was engaged to be married to a Guyanese man who lives in Winnipeg. You know what he said? You are just a child! How could your parents do that? I told him that it was an arranged marriage and I did not want to go but I cannot run away because my family will bring me back home. Nani and Nana think that it is a good thing but my life will be over. They were proud because I am the first grandchild to be getting married. Nani even took me to the jewellery store to buy me a gold bracelet. I will have no friends and no family and I will miss Bena and Karran. We do everything together even when I am sometimes angry at Bena for listening to Portia Faces Life on the radio instead of doing her sweeping or making the beds.

Mr. Ferguson gave me his telephone number so when I arrive in Winnipeg, he can come to visit me. When I gave him the address where I will be living, he said that it was about ten minutes from his apartment. I have never had a teacher come to my house to visit. He said that it is okay with CUSO who sent him to Guyana that he should go back to Canada early. Last year when he was talking about Winnipeg, I was trying to imagine what it was like. In a few weeks I will be living there with some strangers if someone doesn't kill me before I get there. I am glad I asked all those questions. I think God sent him to Cumming's Lodge to look out for me. I bought dark sunglasses but that is not much of a disguise. I wonder who could hate me that much to send me letters threatening to kill me. What if they succeed? Pappy said that it is someone who is not right in their mind and he thinks he knows who it is but he won't tell me. I am so frightened that I can hardly breathe or sleep at night. I have headaches from thinking about this but I am afraid to tell anyone. Every night I pray to God to listen to me and save me from going to Canada. I don't want to die at 16 and it's bad enough to keep a secret about my engagement so I don't get expelled, but to keep a secret about someone wanting to kill me is even worse. I don't know what to do or who to ask for help.

Dear diary,

I am now in Winnipeg with Mommy. We arrived in Canada on July 20th and we stayed in Toronto with Uncle Gun's brother-in-law. I have never seen a place that big. He took us to Niagara Falls and it was the most beautiful thing I've seen. After a few days, we left Toronto by train to come to Winnipeg. This country is so big that I can't believe that we travelled for almost 1400 miles and it only took 30 hours. The conductor on the train was very nice and Mommy said that I was so tired that I was sleeping when the train stopped and the conductor stayed with me the whole time to make sure I was safe.

Diary, I am tired because I am not sleeping at night. I am more scared than ever to come to Winnipeg because Pappy thinks he knows who is writing the letters and it is someone close to

Robin. How could it be that someone would be so cruel? I wore my large sunglasses when I got off the plane but that is not a disguise at all. Mommy and I are staying with Robin's family because we don't know anyone in Winnipeg where we can stay until I get married next week. I don't know these people and as soon as I am married, Mommy is planning to leave the next day. I am afraid to eat because I think someone will poison the food. I am afraid to go outside because I think someone will shoot me. I am just afraid of everything these days but I remain silent about it because I have no one to help.

Robin and I went to the doctor today to talk about birth control. The doctor was asking me some questions about IUDs and pills and I had no idea what he was saying. I have not even thought about that. When I could not answer the questions, the doctor realized that I did not know what he was saying so he started talking to Robin as if he would understand more. I don't know if he does, but I am not going to ask him. I realize now that Mommy should have told me something about this but we have never even talked about me getting my period a few years ago so this is even more private. What if I get pregnant and have a baby when I am 17? What if I can't go back to school? After I left the doctor's office, I had something else to be frightened about

Dear diary,

Saturday was August 1st and it was my wedding day. You know how girls always talk about their wedding as if it is the most important day in their lives? Well, I used to think that mine would be that way but after the last year, I just want to live long enough to tell someone about it. I knew exactly 6 people at my wedding – Mommy, Mr. Ferguson, my uncle and aunt, Kapil and Susheela. Everyone else was a stranger. No father. No sister. No brother. No aunts and uncles. No cousins. No grand-parents. Just strangers. Mommy left the day after I got married. Mr. Ferguson was crying after the ceremony. The minister said some words but I don't remember what they were because I wasn't paying attention. I missed Daddy and Karran but mostly I miss Bena. I felt sad that they weren't here but mostly I felt scared that mommy was going to leave and I would be all alone.

We had no money for a honeymoon like people in Canada have but I don't care. We don't have honeymoons in Guyana anyway. The Lunings lent us their cottage for a few days. It's not really a cottage but an add-on piece that they call an annex. It had a very lumpy bed and was a bit cold but it was fine. In a way, I was glad to be there because I thought the person trying to kill me would not do it while I was here. I am waiting to die and hoping that I don't. Is this the way to start my life in Canada?

Dear diary,

Mr. Ferguson said that I could call him Jim and if I need anything, I can call but I feel strange to call him Jim so I keep calling him Mr. Ferguson or sometimes I talk to him but I don't call his name. He is the only person I know here in Winnipeg.

My mother-in-law had a shower for me before the wedding but I didn't know anyone there. Mommy was talking to some of the women but I did not say one word. Diary, that was hard for me.

It's strange to have a husband and be living in a house with all those strangers. I don't even know how to act. I am not sure if my mother-in-law likes me and my father-in-law hardly talks to me. My young brother-in-law Anand is only six and he likes to spend time with me so that helps me to be not so lonely. Padi is twelve but she looks very grown up. Robin works a lot and he'll be starting his third year of Engineering so I am going to spend a lot more time alone. Chandra and I will be going to school together but he'll be in Grade 12 and I will be in Grade 11. There are seven of us in the house and there is not much privacy. Sometimes I just want a place to go and cry but I can't even do that because Anand comes looking for me.

When I was in Guyana, I felt that I knew so many things but there are so many more things I don't know here even when they should be the same. I long for some mangoes and pineapple but the grocery store over here is so different. They don't have any of that. I even sound different. People say I have an accent but I think they have the accent. I wonder if this is how Mr. Ferguson felt when he went to Guyana. He used to say that root beer tasted great but when he took Mommy and I to A and W to taste it, it tasted like Iodex. I don't know how to act around Robin. I have never even undressed in front of Bena but now I am expected to undress in front of him. My life is changing and I don't like it. I just want to go back home but I have no money to go back. I have written about six letters to my friends but the mail takes so long, I probably won't hear from them till Christmas. I wonder what they are doing and if they think of me. I am always thinking of them and I am so lonely without Bena sleeping next to me at night.

Dear diary,

I started Grade 11 at Vincent Massey Collegiate a month ago. I didn't get my GCE results from Guyana in time for school to start so the principal decided that I had to start in Grade 11. This is the second time in my life that I have to repeat a form or they say grade in Canada. When I was at Belair School I finished Form 1 and when I passed Common Entrance when I was eleven, I had to start in Form 1 at Cumming's Lodge because I was too young to be in Form 2. If I got my GCE results before starting school over here, I might be in Grade 12 but I have to be in Grade 11. I don't mind though because there are so many changes to my life right now that at least if I am doing subjects that I already know, I can do well in school and I can still finish high school when I am 18.

The school is so big and I keep getting lost. There are so many students and I don't know anyone except Chandra. I didn't even know how to read the timetable on the wall and I didn't know how to open the lock on my combination lock. I kept forgetting where my locker was because it's in a different section of the school. They had freshie week and some students wanted to freshie me but Chandra told them that they are not allowed to do that to me. I don't even know what freshie week is. I don't know how to play baseball or soccer or hockey and the volleyball teams are already picked so I can't even play volleyball. Everything is so different. They have intermurals and I never heard that word. At least I don't have to be scared that I am married and in Grade 11. When I registered for school, we told the counsellor and she said that it would be no problem for me to be at school.

I miss my family terribly and I am always scared that the person who sent me the anonymous letters will try to kill me. I try not to look scared but sometimes I can feel my heart beating very fast when I get frightened. I have no friends, no money, no privacy and worse than that, I have no family. I feel abandoned. I feel scared and anxious all the time and I just want to go home back to my old life. I am crying so much that I think that I will never stop. I lock myself in the bathroom and have a shower and cry there so no one will see me. I feel that I am turning into a different person being married and living with strangers. I don't know how to act and I feel like I will never smile again. In Guyana, when I was scared about things, I always knew Daddy and Mommy were there but here is not the same. Robin's parents are not like my parents so I cannot go to them when I am not feeling well.

At the start of school, my gym teacher said that I had to get a pair of shorts for gym. I told Robin and he said that I could get one but we had to be careful with our money since he still has two more years of engineering at the university and he only works in the summer so our money has to last for a long time. I don't know how much money he has but I have none and I won't ask him for any. I found a pair of shorts for $6 at Young Togs but I was not sure if that was a lot of money since Mommy always bought my clothes. Diary, this is the first time that I don't have any money and my dad isn't here to ask me if I have enough and to give me more if I don't.

Our bedroom is in the basement and it's always so cold down there. There is hardly any sunlight in the room except for about 10 minutes in the morning through the basement window. I miss my huge backyard where I learned to ride my bike. I miss my friends and my life and I just want to go home but I know that is not possible. I wouldn't even have money for the plane ticket. I wonder if I will ever see Guyana again. Daddy said that Canada was a better life but it's worse in every way. I have no family, I have no friends, I don't know the games at school, I don't know how to act in the lunch room and I still keep getting lost in some parts of the school.

The very worst part of school is English. I have a terrible English teacher. He hates me and tries to find every chance to embarrass me. At Massey, I have a home room where the teacher takes our attendance. In Guyana, we stay in our classrooms all day and the teachers come to our room but here at Massey, I have to go to a different classroom for each subject after we leave our home room in the morning. On the first day of class, I got lost and arrived late to English class. Mr. Henderson was standing by his desk and the only seat that was left was at the front right next to his desk. I sat down and realized that I left my purse in my homeroom desk. I told him that I forgot my purse in my home room. He stared at me and acted like he didn't understand what I was saying. He kept looking at me as if I was a dunce so after I repeated it two more times, he announced to the class: Does anyone know what she is saying? I could see the other students sitting near to me felt bad for me but no one said anything. My face turned red so I picked up his chalk and went over to the chalkboard and wrote the word PURSE. He looked at the word and said something like: Oh, perse; I thought you said fourth. I don't know how purse could sound like fourth. He said that I should learn to speak proper English. I who come from an English speaking country should learn to speak English! I who had great marks in English in Mr. Johnson's class was told that I should learn to speak English! I have not said another word in his class since then and you know how hard it is for me not to talk diary. I am always so nervous when I walk into his class. It is so unlike Mr. Johnson's literature class in Guyana. He was kind and caring and Mr. Henderson is nasty and mean but he only does that to me. He doesn't even look at me when he talks to me. He just talks at the side of his shoulder as if he can't bear to look at me.

Mrs. Houston is so different. She is my home room teacher and she is so kind. Sometimes I like to think of her as my mom but I don't actually say that to her. Susan Singleton sits beside me and she wears thick glasses. She doesn't have many friends but she talks to me so I am happy since she is the only one in my class who does. We are partners in gym class but I think it's because no one wants to be her partner and the other students don't talk to me. Miss Parker the physical education teacher told us that we had to pick a song and do a modern dance to it. I have no idea what modern dance is. Susan showed me how and we had to interpret the song through dance. We did a really stupid dance. It doesn't look anything like the Indian dances we do or even the English dances we did when mommy and daddy had parties. We used to listen to Elvis and did Jailhouse Rock and the twist with Chubby Checker but I don't understand what modern dance is. It looked so silly that I wanted to laugh but everyone else was already laughing at us so it just felt even more stupid. Sandi Gilmour and Barb Milley are really friendly but they are not in my home room. I met them in my English class and they think that Mr. Henderson is horrible to me. They said I should tell Mr. Sotolov the principal or Mr. Trainor the vice principal but at home you only go the office if you are in trouble so it's best if I stay away from the office. Mr. Ackland the biology teacher is also very nice and so is Mr. Smallwood the Geography teacher. Well really all my teachers are nice except Mr. Henderson. I am doing well in all my courses except English and I thought that would be my best course. I am even doing very well in Miss Wilkinson's Mathematics class so that is a big thanks to Mr. Ferguson. Miss Wilkinson knows Mr. Ferguson but I think it might be from when she went to university.

Dear Diary,

Sandi and Barb invited me to their house for Halloween. I don't know what that is but Sandi explained that you get dressed up in costumes and go to people's house and they give you candies. That is the strangest thing I ever heard. We went over to her house and Mrs. Gilmour showed me how to make candy apples with melted caramel. I helped her make some. Their house smells like baking cookies. They have a nice house and a big dog. I miss my dogs and when I see her mom and dad and her brother laughing and talking to each other, I miss my family.

My in-laws don't talk to each other like that. I mean they don't laugh and talk to each other. They are always serious. When I go home after school, I help out in the kitchen but we don't really talk. Robin is busy at university so he stays late and I hardly see him. There was a dance at Vincent Massey but he didn't want to go because he said that they were all high school students and he was too old for that. When I was at Cumming's Lodge, I used to plan the school dances with the other students. The best one we had was a fashion and talent show. I wore a sari and everyone said I looked like a model. I felt so pretty that day. Now I don't think anyone even notices me and when they do, they just look at me as if there is something wrong with me. The other students laugh and talk with their friends and they sit in the lunch room together and some boys and girls stand at the lockers and kiss. We would never be allowed to do that at Cumming's Lodge. Boys and girls were not even supposed to be talking to each other without other boys and girls around. We could get detention for that and now I see girls standing outside of the school doors smoking cigarettes and the teachers don't say anything. We would have been expelled from school at Cumming's Lodge for getting caught smoking. Or at least you would get a caning.

I was in the bus last week and there was an empty seat beside me. I moved over closer to the window and told the lady that was standing that she could sit next to me. She just looked at me as if she scorned me and kept standing. I know that look. It was the same one that some of the students at Cumming's Lodge used to give to Paulette when she had scabies. Her skin would get red patches and she would be itching all the time. The other students didn't want to sit near her so they avoided her. It was sad because she had other problems too even though her father was a doctor. Her clothes never fit, her hair was chopped off as if someone was sawing her hair and her shoes and socks were scruffy and dirty. I used to pick her for my rounders team because I was the captain of the team even though I knew she couldn't hit a ball but I felt sorry that no one else picked her. She never did anything on the team but I was a good rounders player and the other team members and I could score enough runs to make up for her. She was so glad to be included that she used to wait for me every afternoon to walk out to the public road where mommy would pick me up in the Toyota. I sometimes wished she wouldn't walk with me but I didn't tell her to stop. Eventually I was only going with the train so she had no one to walk with.

That look on the lady's face in the bus was the same. I never had anyone look at me like that in Guyana. Is this what poor Paulette felt like all those times? It's a horrible feeling as if you are dirty and you can't wash yourself off. I hear on the news that white people don't like the natives. Maybe the lady thought I was a native Indian. One of the counsellors in school was praising me for how well I speak English. She said my English is very good and I told her that her English was also good. She said that I was rude and impertinent but I don't understand why. We both speak English so why would she say that my English is good?

1971

Dear dairy,

It's getting colder and the coat I am wearing is not warm. I am always cold these days. My finger tips are cracked and they bleed and it hurts but I don't know how to fix it. I never had dry hands like this. I went to the Eaton's clearance centre and bought a coat for $5. It is green and ugly but it's all I can afford. I'm afraid that if I spend any more, Robin might be angry because we don't have a lot. Daddy sent me some money at Christmas so I bought a watch because I needed one. It's hard to tell the time when it's winter here. It's dark all the time.

Daddy and Mommy called from Guyana and I told them that I am doing well even though I cry most of the time and miss them terribly. I write a lot of letters to my friends. I hope they remember me. Christmas is not the same in Canada as it is in Guyana. I miss going to the store on Christmas Eve with Karran and Bena and Daddy. Robin and his family don't really celebrate Christmas. For them it's a time to exchange presents but we used to go to church for Christmas Eve mass. My mother-in-law is Hindu so she says that she doesn't celebrate Christmas. I'm glad we used to celebrate Christmas even though Daddy is Hindu and Mommy is Muslim – well sort of. She converted to a Christian and Karran, Bena and I were all baptized as Christians.

Some of my friends think that we don't really belong anywhere but I think I am lucky that we belong everywhere. We get celebrate Hindu, Muslim and Christian holidays.

Dear diary,

It's February and the winter is worse than I thought. I remember the first day in October when I saw a few snowflakes and I was so excited until someone said it was snow flurries. The first snow fall was fun but it is now endless cold days and my fingers are all cracked and bleeding from walking to and from school 4 times each day. The ten minute walk to school is now feeling like ten hours. I don't have proper clothes but I don't want to ask for more because we have so little money. I need long pants and thick stocking but all I have are thin stockings and skirts so my knees are always frozen by the time walk to and from school four times each day. This is the first time that I need something and I can't have it and I have no one to ask or buy it for me.

Today is Daddy's birthday. Yesterday was my 17th birthday and for the first time in my life, I did not celebrate it with him. I used to long to have my own birthday cake but now I have none. It's the worst birthday that I ever spent. Robin bought me a sweater and I think he is trying to cheer me up, but it's not the same. I'm just lonely. I have two or three friends at Massey but we don't really spend any time together after school because they are involved with sports activities that I don't know how to play. They live in the opposite direction of me and I don't know how to get to Sandy's house without getting lost coming back home so I don't go. She also swims and skis so she is busy most weekends. Robin doesn't like to do things at my high school because he is older. I went with him to a beer bash at the university but I don't drink and his friends think that I am too young anyway. These days I don't seem to fit in anywhere. I just stay at home in my room because I am afraid that if I am out when it's dark, the person who wanted to kill me might do so.

Dear diary,

Last weekend Robin and I went to an Indian movie that was showing at the university. The Indian students from India sponsor the movie. When I was in Guyana, I loved to go to the movies and almost every weekend, Sister Khemo would come and she and Bena and I would go to see an Indian movie. I don't understand Hindi but all the movies have subtitles so they are easy to follow. Most movies have beautiful songs and I love to listen to them on the radio or at weddings. I was very excited to do something like that. I wore a nice dress but it was still cold because we have to go by bus and it's a long way to walk to the bus stop. I didn't even mind the cold because Robin said that there will be a lot of Indian people at the movies so maybe I could make some new friends who are similar to us. That was the most disappointing experience for me. None of the Indian people would talk to us after they introduced themselves in Hindi and we could not answer them in Hindi.

Afterwards, one of the Indian men said that most people from India think that Indian people who are not from India are not real Indians because they left the motherland for green pastures. That is not true for most Indian people in Guyana. Most of my ancestors went to Guyana as indentured labourers because the British government promised that they would make lots of money and they could return to India. But the British did not pay them their wages so they could not go back. Many of them stayed in Guyana and would not talk about those times. I wish I could tell the other Indians from India that they are wrong but some of them are professors so they are much smarter than I am.

Dear diary,

I got my first summer job in Canada. I am working at a factory making frost shields for cars. It's on Gomez Street off of Higgins. It's not hard work but it pays good money. I am glad that I am only doing it for the summer. I wouldn't want to do this for a living because it's boring and the supervisor is not nice but I don't say anything to cause any trouble. I stay at my table and work quickly attaching the wires to the plastic so Frank's mom said that I could do piece work and get paid a bit more. I started working faster and now I am earning extra money. She and some of the older ladies come from Eastern Europe and they do this for a living but they don't work fast so they don't get the extra for piece work. They hardly speak English so this is the only kind of work that they can get. She said that people from Eastern Europe are not treated nicely especially the ones from Poland. I don't know which ones are from Poland. They all look white to me. I am brown so it's easy for people to see that I am different.

I am going to work hard to save some money to go to hairdressing school when I finish high school. I'm not really interested in university so I asked my counsellor at Massey about hairdressing and she said that if I want to do that, I have to go to RB Russell School in downtown. It would take me more than one hour each way to school and home and Robin said that it is not a safe area of the city. He used to live on Manitoba Avenue and they moved to Fort Garry so this is not a good plan besides he wants me to go to university so I am taking university entrance courses. If I go to RB, I won't be able to do that and do hairdressing because the timetable will be different and besides, I will have to make new friends all over again. I really only have two friends at Massey anyway but going to RB Russell will be worse because I won't live in the same neighbourhood as the other students and at the end of the day, I won't be able to go to anyone's house without coming home very late. So I'll finish high school and use my summer money to go to hairdressing school. Every day I pass the Pollock Beauty School on Graham so I might go there.

I am saving all my money. I pass the ice-cream shop every day and I see that a cone is still 10 cents but I don't spend any of my money because I am afraid that if I do that, I'll buy one every day and at the end of the week, I'll have 50 cents less money. I am so scared of spending any money because it may run out. Imagine that when I was in Guyana I used to buy whatever I wanted and if I didn't have money, I would use the shop book and daddy would pay for it but now I won't even buy an ice-cream cone for ten cents. My friends at Massey think that I am rich because I always have $5 but it's the same $5 each week. They get an allowance every week and they spend it on canned spaghetti and cigarettes and licorice but I don't spend mine on anything so they think that because I am married I get lots of money. I am becoming a miser and I'm embarrassed to ask Robin for money. He has a worse job because he works in a fibreglass factory and he comes home very itchy every day. His university friends have family and other friends who offer them summer jobs in engineering offices but he doesn't know anyone like that, so he works in the fibreglass factory. Same with his cousin Susheela. She is very bright but she doesn't know anyone who can offer her a job in an office so she works at the factory with me to pay her university fees. Robin thinks that she will get the gold medal from her faculty when she graduates from the university but she works in a factory during the summer. I know she is very bright. She used to live next door to me and Pappy is her father and when I was younger, she loved to read and would go under her bed and read there for a long time. She was my bridesmaid at our wedding.

1972

Dear diary,

It's been a long time since I wrote you. I graduated from Massey and even though I saved almost all my money, we don't have enough for me to go to hairdressing school so I am working at a Safeway. I didn't apply to university because I really wanted to go to hairdressing school at Red River Community College or at Pollock Beauty School but we don't have the tuition money so I wouldn't have been able to go anyway. I am glad to be finished high school and it is a terrible disappointment not to be able to do hairdressing.

Grade 12 English class all year was horrible with Mr. Henderson because he always made me feel so stupid in his class. I got him again in Grade 12 English and he treated me the same as he did all through Grade 11 as if I am retarded. He never talked to me all year and it didn't matter how hard I tried, I could not get a higher mark than between 50 and 52 on his tests. I thought I was going to fail English but I exempted all my courses and didn't have to write any final exams with good marks except for English which I passed with 52%. I'll miss some of the other teachers though. Mrs. Houston asked if I was going to university or college but I told her that I wouldn't have enough money for the fees. I had one or two good experiences in school though. One of the counsellors asked me to represent Massey at a Model United Nations at Red River Community College. I don't really belong to the school club but they thought that since I am coloured, I would be a good representative for the Republic of the Congo so I went. It was interesting but I didn't really understand a lot of it because I don't know anything about the United Nations or the Congo.

I applied to Safeway as a cashier but they had no jobs for that so I said that I would take anything so I'm working as a meat wrapper in the meat department. It's hard work lifting the heavy trays of meat but I can manage it. I'm a hard worker and I am fast so although I am only casual, I'm getting almost 30-35 hours each week. I still want to do hairdressing so I am not spending any of my money. I bring my own lunch and save as much as I can so that I can go to school. I don't want to be a professional meat wrapper. The butchers are all men and they get paid a lot but mostly women are wrappers and they don't get paid nearly as much and they work just as hard.

I used to work at Payfair as a cashier when I graduated but it was hard to work seven days a week. I got two days off at Payfair but on one of the days off I worked at another Payfair and on Sundays I worked at Leslie's Grocery during the day and Robin worked there in the evening. We hardly see each other. Robin graduated from the University of Manitoba in May as a Mechanical Engineer and he spent the whole summer looking for work but he couldn't find work as an engineer so he worked with one of his professors doing some work at Pinawa and part-time as a gardener and then part-time at Leslie's. Most of his friends got hired by their parents or family friends who have engineering companies but he isn't so lucky. He saw an advertisement in the newspaper for an engineering job but when he went to the company to fill out the application, the secretary said that the job was already taken. He came home and called the company and the same secretary said that the position is still available. We think that it's because he was not white that they didn't want to hire him but there are some people who are nice to us. He finally got a job in September at MCW but his boss expects him to work very long hours and doesn't pay any overtime. Sometimes he comes home at 1 or 2 am.

I sponsored my parents to come to Canada but life here is not as good as daddy said it would be. He said that I would have more opportunities in Canada but so far, I have a high school diploma and I am a meat wrapper in a grocery store. Bena said that Daddy's trucking business is doing well even though he has to bribe a lot of people but he is getting work. Burnham is not ruling the country very well so it's getting harder for Indians to live there. I don't know what they will do in Canada because working as a meat wrapper and gardener is not the life I thought I was going to have.

Dear diary,

Well Robin finally got a job at an engineering firm. He is working as a draftsman at MCW but his boss is taking advantage because he knows that Robin doesn't have other choices. He gets $400 each month which is much lower than most engineers make but he hopes that this job will lead to a better one. He doesn't really know how to draft because he studied to be an engineer for four years but he needed a job badly. His boss told him one day that if he works harder than he is already working, in 15 or 20 years, he could make $50,000. He is already working almost 14 to 16 hours each day!

I hope one day I'll have enough money to go to school and the great life that daddy promised will happen. Life in Canada is not like the Christmas postcard that I used to think it was and I am sure glad that I did not listen to my mom when she used to write and tell me that I should have a baby and send it back to Guyana for them to raise until I finish school. Some Guyanese women do that. They have their babies and they send the baby back to Guyana and bring the baby back when the child is older so the mother and father miss all the baby years. I would never do that. When I have my own baby, I will raise it myself.

1973

Dear diary,

I applied to a hospital to do an operating technician diploma and I got in. Eighty people applied and they only pick 16 and I was one of them. I really want to be a hairdresser but Robin and his dad think that I can do better so instead of nursing which they think I should do or a secretary which I really detest because I dislike typing, I picked something else because I know I don't want to be a nurse. I was supposed to start at the beginning of September but on the last Friday in August, I found out that I am pregnant. I think God must have heard me praying for a miracle. This is my miracle because it means that I don't have to go and do that. I was vomiting so much that I wouldn't be able to go to school and stand for long hours and I won't be able to complete the program before the baby comes in March. I can't even go back to work at Safeway because I have to lift heavy trays and the smell of raw meat makes me even more sick.

I bought a portable Singer's sewing machine for $89 and I am teaching myself to sew. I took Home Ec. at Massey but I didn't really learn to sew or cook because the teacher spent a lot of time with the girls who were planning to go to university to study home Ec. I learned to cook and bake bread and pastries very well in Guyana but we made some awful things in Home Ec. at Massey. I wouldn't eat most of the things we had to cook but the other girls said that they thought the food we made was good. I don't know what they eat but the food had no taste. I never complained because I got good marks. I should show them how to cook some curry or stew fish but they might think I am showing off or they might not like it so I didn't say I already know how to cook very well. I made some nice maternity dresses for myself and I am doing really well with the patterns. I made some baby clothes and can't wait for the baby to come. I got over many months of morning sickness although I don't know why they call it morning sickness when I was sick all day. I am so looking forward to the baby coming because with Robin working so many long hours, I spend a lot of time alone at home. I am reading a lot and sewing and I have the television on all day to make it feel less lonely.

Dear diary,

Robin got a new job at Reid Crowther and Partners. He is now working as an engineer instead of a draftsman. The pay is a bit more than he was making at MCW but his boss is very kind. He started out with $500 each month but he does not have to work for 16 hours each day. I think his new boss felt sorry for him and hired him. His boss needed someone with five years of work experience but hired him with only eight months of work experience.

We saved so much money that we bought a house with three bedrooms. Robin's dad saw the house and he said that the people who are selling it are getting divorced and they are selling it for $20,000 which is only half the price of the house so we put down $5,000 as a down payment. He was surprised that we saved so much money in one year. We only spend money on food and rent so we saved a lot. This means that all the money I was going to save for school went toward buying the house. Well, I didn't want to go to that school anyway so it's just as well that we used the money for something else.

1974

Dear diary,

I now have my baby girl. Her name is Sharmila Savitree and she is the most beautiful baby on this earth. I'm so glad to have her. Now I am not as lonely as I was. My sewing is getting better and made a matching outfit for her and me. I'm getting better with each outfit that I make. I spend a lot of time watching her sleep and playing with her but she is only a baby so she sleeps a lot. I am nursing her but most people at the pre-natal classes that we attended will be using formula. They think that I should do the same but I think it's better if I nurse her. Some people think that I am strange but the LaLeche League thinks that I should breast feed her because it will give her a good start to her life. To be a mother at 20 is hard because everyone wants to give me advice and I want to do what my heart tells me is the right thing even when it's opposite of what everyone else is saying.

Dear diary,

I enrolled at Herzing College to take a correspondence diploma in computer programming. Robin comes home late every night and he even works on the weekends and Sharmi is a good baby so I have time to study when she is sleeping. The course isn't hard and I am getting good marks but it is so boring. I think my dream of being a hairdresser will not come true so I'm going to study hard to be a programmer. I used to dream that one day I would have my own salon and I would create beautiful hairstyles but that's not to be, so this is for the best. Diary, I am only saying that but I don't really believe it is for the best. It is disappointing to think that I want something so badly and it won't happen. Mommy and Daddy are getting through with their papers to come to Canada so when they arrive, I'll ask them to babysit so I can go back to school.

I have not heard anything from any of my friends at Massey. They must be in university and going on ski trips like they did in high school. I am glad that I have someone to take care of and university doesn't interest me but I would be really happy if one of them called. I don't know any other young mothers so I spend a lot of time by myself taking care of Sharmi and studying. Sometimes I used to make some noise so she'd wake up because the house is so quiet, but now that I am studying, it's not so bad. I am getting really good marks but I just wish it that the course wasn't so boring. I cannot imagine doing this for the rest of my life but this is it. At least I'll have an education.

1975

Dear diary,

My parents came over a few months ago in September. I was so happy to see them. I got a new sister Sophie since I left Guyana. She was born in 1972 so she is just 15 months older than Sharm. They had to look for an apartment to live in because they could not afford to rent a house for the five of them. Most landlords don't want to rent to five people and there are hardly any three bedroom apartments that they can afford. They found a two bedroom one that they liked but they had to tell the landlord that there were only four of them and that Sophie is my daughter.

Mr. Fultz is the landlord and he has an office on the second floor just a few doors down from my parents' apartment. He sees Sophie there every day and she calls mom "mommy" I am sure he knows she is not my daughter but he doesn't say anything because he likes her and he brings candy for her. Daddy got a job at Creamette's. They make spaghetti and macaroni noodles. He doesn't like it and it doesn't pay good money but he needed work right away so he took the first job that he could get. Mom and Dad asked Mr. Fultz if they could get a job with him cleaning the offices in his building. These are my parents who had servants in Guyana and my mom who never went anywhere without shoes on her feet and now they are washing toilets for a living.

When they left Guyana, Burnham's government would not allow them to take more than $15 US dollars each so they had to find work right away. Mom is working in the evenings at Ringers Drug store and Bena is working at Great West Life as a secretary. Karran is at Massey and he is in the naval reserve part-time so he can earn some spending money. This is my family that had a good life in Guyana and my dad is now working as a labourer in a macaroni factory. It was so good though to be reunited and finally we had a Christmas like I remember in Guyana with all my family around me.

I got awfully sick on Old Year's night and I had to go to the hospital for surgery to have my gall stones removed. I had a gallstone attack just after my parents arrived in Winnipeg but I wanted to spend my first Christmas with them after four long years so I told the doctor that I would wait until after the new year for my surgery. It was very painful before Christmas when I had bouts of pain but it was worth the pain to be with every-one for the holidays. It took me two months to recover from the surgery but mommy and Bena helped with Sharmi for a week after I came out of the hospital. I have a very ugly scar down the front of my stomach but I have no more pain from the gall stones.

I did something last week that I am excited about but Robin and my parents are not pleased with me. I asked Mom and Dad if they would take care of Sharm so I could go back to school to study and they said yes. I didn't tell anyone about my plan but I went downtown to Pollock Beauty School and registered and paid my fees for the hairdressing program. I paid $350 for the full tuition. I came home and told them and they were not happy. They thought I was going to sign up at Herzing to do the computer programming so I let them think that was what I was going to do. I only told them after I came home because I knew they would talk me out of it. Bena said that she can't imagine washing people's dirty hair for a living but I think of all the beautiful hairstyles I can create.

Dear diary,

It's been several months since I started hairdressing school. I love the smell of a salon and I love doing hair. I don't think I have been this happy in a long time – except for when my family came to Canada. Mr. Pollock said that I have to cut my hair short if I expect to be a hairdresser. My hair is down to my bum and I told him that I am not cutting it but I will specialize in long hair styles and the long hair clients can come to me. The other students don't like to do long hair so I get all the long hair clients. It was a good decision because my long hair attracts a lot of people because it's shiny and healthy.

Robin finally got over being upset with me for signing up for hairdressing school because he sees how well I am doing and how much I love it. My marks are more than 90% on my theory tests and I know that I am doing better than most of the other students. Mom and Bena come to the school for me to practice. Sometimes Robin brings Sharm to pick me up at night. We bought a brand new car just before my parents came to Canada. Mr. Pollock is very good to me. Every Monday and Wednesday he stays open late for the part-time evening students so I asked if I could stay and earn extra hours. I have to complete 1400 hours so he agreed and he even makes supper for the students because most of them are working in factories during the day and don't have time to eat dinner before coming to classes. I was hoping to complete my program in 8 or 9 months rather than one year but I had to take two months off in the summer because Mom had surgery and she could not take care of Sharm. I should still be done by December or January.

Diary did I say Mr. Pollock is a good man? Well he is. He yells a lot at the students but he doesn't really mean anything. One time when I first started, one of the clients didn't want me to do her hair because I was a "darkie" – that's what she called me – so she pulled out the rollers and told Mr. Pollock that I was sloppy. He came and yelled at me in front of all the other students so I packed up my things and told him that I was not going to have him be disrespectful to me and I left. I was shaking when I said that and I cried all the way home on the bus. The next day he called and said he was sorry and I should come back because I was a good student so I went back and since then he has been really kind. Sometimes he gives me a ride home with some of the other students because it's dark by the time we leave school at night. He helps out Kim because she doesn't have a lot of money. He said that life was hard for him as a Jew when he was young so he wants to help other people if he can. Sometimes I hear the students saying bad things about him because he is a Jew but I am not sure why Jews are bad. I don't think we had Jews in Guyana but I don't know for sure.

I am learning a lot from him and some of it is not even related to hair. Two months ago he asked if anyone had a driver's licence and I said that I had one so he gave me his car and asked me to go to a client's house to do her hair because she was a shut-in. So I started going each week and he told me to keep the money that she paid to get her hair done. I said it was his money and his gas but he said that I deserve it. He only charges her what he charges the clients who come to the school which is almost nothing. I think it is so good for him to help people who have it hard. I may do that when I graduate. There must be a lot of people who can't go to the salon because they have little kids at home or they are in wheelchairs or too sick to go out. With the tips and the money that I get to go out to clients, I will be able to recover all my tuition. So far, I made back most of my tuition money in tips and most clients only leave 25 cents so you can figure out how many clients I work on every day to make back $300 already.

Dear diary,

I am getting very good at doing hair especially long hair. I love it so much that every morning when I go to school, I go straight to my station and start working on my clients. I am booked up all day with clients and they are requesting me to do their hair. I have to tell you something funny. Remember the time I was trying to smoke the squash vine when I was little? Well at school, a lot of the students smoke. In the mornings when I come to school, one of the teachers and some of the students sit in the lunch room or sometimes upstairs in the client waiting area and smoke. They are always laughing and chatting so one day I decided that I wanted to fit in with them so I was going to start smoking too. I asked Judy to buy a cigarette from her and the whole crowd of students started shouting at me that I should not do that. At first I was surprised that they were shouting but they said that I should never start smoking because it was a bad habit and they thought I was too good to be doing something so bad. One of them said that she forbid me to smoke because I was a good person from a decent family she would not let me ruin my life. That was a big surprise because they don't really know anything about my family or my life.

Later when I asked her what she meant, she said that the way I dress and speak and the way I work so hard, she knows I should be doing something better than hairdressing. She asked me if I finished high school and I said yes that I graduated with a university entrance Grade 12. She asked why I didn't go to university and I said I wasn't interested in university; I only wanted to be a hairdresser. She said that she doesn't want to be a hairdresser but she did not finish high school so she has to work with her hands. She said that she lives in the North End and many of her friends dropped out of school and cannot find work.

She said that her older sister is a hairdresser and the pay is not good and the working conditions are not good because many salon owners treat the employees badly or don't pay them well. If her sister doesn't have any clients for that day, the owner will send her home with no pay and she can't complain because she'll be fired. I told her that I wouldn't have to worry about that because I was going to have my own salon when I could afford it and if I hire people, I will be good to them like daddy was when he had some of the poor men working on his truck. She said that was the difference between us – that she hated being a hairdresser and she would never be able to afford to have her own salon. I didn't know what to say. Sometimes diary, I can talk a lot and sometimes I have no words when people say some things. I just have a lot of thoughts in my head for days that make me think. I don't know why but Salim came into my thoughts. I wonder if he wanted to sell sugar cakes at Belair School or if he had to do that because his family was poor.

1976

Dear diary,

I graduated as a hairdresser in March. Now people are calling us hairstylists so I have to remember to say that. I got a job at Tony's Barber shop. He owns a salon and a barber shop but he can't hire me for the barber shop because I need a barber licence so he said that if the inspector comes in, I have to say that I am working in the salon. It's weird that if I live in Winnipeg or Brandon I must have a hairdresser or barber licence but if I live anywhere else in the province, I can work as a barber or hairdresser without any skills or education. That doesn't make the least bit of sense. I only stayed at Tony's for a few months because I am now expecting my second baby and I have awful morning sickness which lasts all day. The smell of anything sweet bothers me so shampoo and hairspray makes me even more sick. I don't mind staying home though. I didn't like the nursery school that Sharm is going to so now I can stay home and take care of her while I wait for the next baby. We sold the house on Waller for twice the money that we bought it for three years ago and we bought a brand new house in Waverley Heights. I give free haircuts to the neighbours and to family so I am still doing hair but I just don't get paid.

Oh diary, I forgot to tell you this funny story. When I finished the program at Pollock's Beauty School, Mr. Pollock's daughter Karen told me that she remembered when I came to the school last year to sign up for the program and she and Cindy and some other students made bets with each other that I would not last one month in the program, let alone graduate. I was surprised that she would think so because I worked very hard and I was dedicated. She said that I didn't look like the typical hairdressing student because I was dressed very nice and I was too groomed to be a hairdresser. They didn't think that I would be able to stand all day and she admitted that she thought I had never done any hard work in my entire life. I should have told her about all the chickens I had to kill and pluck for daddy's business. I guess diary that she doesn't know me like you do. When I want something badly enough, I can be very determined and this was the one thing that I wanted so badly that I was willing to work as hard as I needed to in order to succeed.

1978

Dear diary,

You must have really missed me. Sunita Natasha was born in August last year and I was so busy taking care of two daughters that I had no time to write. Dad and mom celebrated their twenty-fifth wedding anniversary in December and they are also celebrating two years since they bought their house on North Drive. We had the party at our new house. They are very happy about their house but they are still cleaning for Mr. Fultz. He is really good to them.

I love being a mother and taking care of the children but I miss having an adult to talk to. My sewing has gotten so much better. I made some maternity clothes for me and some little outfits for Sharm and Sunita. I give them the latest children's haircuts and I am getting lots of practice doing the neighbours hair for free. Our house is so beautiful. We have four bedrooms and it smells so new! The kitchen is very big and so is the backyard. I am planting a garden with lots of vegetables so that's keeping me busy too. We live across the street from a community centre so when the girls are big enough, they can do some activities at the club. Sharmi is going to a nursery school close to Mom's home but since I don't have a car, Bobby's mom kindly offered to take her with her car because he goes to the same nursery school. I also enrolled her in beginner's piano lessons but we can't afford a piano so she plays on a cardboard keyboard. I shouldn't call it playing because there is no sound but I plan to buy a piano when we can afford it. Now that I have my own children, I can see why dad thought education was so important. He did not get to finish high school in Guyana because his dad died and his uncle who became his step father made him leave school to take care of his younger sisters and brothers. Anyway, he is very smart because he reads a lot and had two successful businesses in Guyana. He used to tell us that he is self-educated but that is a hard way to get an education so he wanted a better life for us. When he came to Canada, he went to school while he was working to get his GED. He is so proud of that accomplishment. He wanted to get some further education but he cannot afford to do that and pay a mortgage and take care of his family.

Diary, I forgot to mention that Mom and I went back to Guyana because Nani was very sick. It was the first time in almost eight years since I left Guyana and things have changed a lot since I left in 1970. Everything looks old and dingy and people are complaining that the government favours black people and many Indian families are leaving to go to the US or Canada. They said that the British caused the racial fights between the Negroes and the Indians and then they left Guyana in a mess after independence. I spent a lot of time with Nana talking about family and I wrote down all the family information he gave me so that I could start a family tree when I came back to Canada. Nana and Nani had twelve children so I have lots of aunts, uncles and cousins and that's not even counting dad's side of the family. If I don't start writing down all the names that they are telling me, I won't remember who all my family are and living in Canada, it will be easier to forget. I have already forgotten some of the names of the streets in Georgetown but I didn't know them well before I left Guyana.

Dear dairy,

Since Robin got the engineering job at Reid Crowther, he seems to be busier than before so he is hardly ever at home. I am really raising the girls by myself. In January I told him that I was going to look for a job as a hairstylist for Saturdays only because I need some adult company and some mental stimulation and he agreed to babysit one day a week if I found a job. I went out and found a job at the first place I looked. Orion Hair Design is only about ten minutes to walk from home. Robin thought I wouldn't find a job and he wouldn't have to babysit so he was not pleased at all. He said that it would cost him more in taxes if I worked than if I stayed home but I wouldn't give in so he stays home on Saturdays. It's more work for me to work one day a week because he doesn't do any house work or cooking when I am away and as soon as I come home, I have to take over looking after the children. I don't like it but I am not going to quit because I love it and Erica and Sylvia are good to me. They told me that I should go on commission because I'll make about $100 each Saturday rather than the $48 that I would make on hourly wages. I'm also getting to know some people in the neighbourhood.

Diary, I forgot to tell you about this. I was reading through the newspaper a few months ago and the YWCA was advertising a program for young mothers so I went to a meeting and we have now started a group called Waverley Heights Y Neighbours. It's for young mothers and there are twelve of us. The first meeting was at my house and we plan the weekly topics that we want to discuss. I met my best friend Catherine at that first meeting. After we talked to each other for a few minutes, we found out that we have a lot in common. We share the same ocean when we were growing up – except that she lived in Newfoundland and I lived in Guyana. We both like salt fish cakes and we both like and miss the smell of salt ocean air.

All of us take our pre-school children to the community club across the street and we hired a babysitter for the two hours that we meet each week. We don't really have a lot of money so we are holding bake and garage sales to raise money to help pay for the babysitting costs. It's fun and interesting; we invite guest speakers on all kinds of topics and it's good to meet other mothers in the community who share similar interests. The only meeting I didn't like was the one about how to be the Perfect Wife. The speaker said that the man is the head of the household and the wives should not be bothering the husband with child rearing stories when he comes home because he is tired. Instead we should by greeting him at the door at the end of his work day by wrapping ourselves in nothing more than plastic wrap and we should make sure the children stay out of his way so he can rest because he was out all day earning money for the family. That meeting was at my house and I felt bad that I was so rude to the guest speaker but the entire speech was such drivel that I could not contain myself so I was very rude to her. Sydney was upset because she invited the speaker who goes to her church. I told her that if I did what the speaker suggested, Robin would think that I went mad – if he was the one at the door when I opened it. The other women didn't say anything when she was speaking but after she left, they cheered and said I was a women's libber. I spend all day taking care of the kids and she said something stupid like that as if my contribution has no value. Catherine and I laughed about it for weeks after but Sydney would not speak to me at the other meetings.

1979

Dear diary,

Sharmi is now in French Immersion kindergarten. Last Spring I was talking to some of the women in Y Neighbours and we thought that it would be good for our children to be bilingual so we should ask the Fort Garry School Division to start a kindergarten. A few of the parents and I petitioned them to start one. The school board said no initially and after we wouldn't give up, they said that unless we had at least 15 students, they wouldn't do it. We spent most of the summer encouraging parents of Kindergarten and Grade 1 kids to sign the petition for a French Immersion school in the division. Some parents that we approached were quite hostile and said that French people get too many privileges so they are not in favour of such a school. We tried to explain that the parents who want a French Immersion school are not French speakers. We want our children to learn French because Canada is bilingual and learning a second language would provide more opportunities for them when they grow up but we couldn't convince them.

Lucky for us that we got 15 students for kindergarten and 15 for Grade 1 so the school division was obliged to provide French Immersion according to government legislation. I didn't know too much about that but some of the parents are very educated so they explained the legislation to those who did not know. The board then told us that they didn't have space for the program so the parents had to search and found some space in a junior high school. The school board decided to put the little kids in a section of General Byng which is a junior

high school. We agreed but only if the little kids had a different start and finish time than the junior high kids. Then they
said that they would not be able to hire French teachers because
there are none available. Imagine that St Boniface is the largest
French speaking community outside of Quebec and the school
division can't find French speaking teachers. Then they didn't
want to start a French library for the kids. The final roadblock
was when they said that they would not provide bussing and
we would either have to drive our kids there or pay for bussing
which is $750 per year. The students who are bussed in the
English programs don't have to pay but when we asked about
that, the school board would not back down. The school division is trying everything not to provide French Immersion. I
can hardly afford the $750 but we found the money because
both Robin and I think that it is very important that our children receive a solid education.

We spent almost the whole summer petitioning and fighting for the program and it is exhausting but I am learning a lot
about how superintendents and school trustees have a great
deal of power over people's lives and how if you don't stand up
to them, they'll walk all over you as my dad says. It's such a fight
to get a good education but I'm not going to give up. Sometimes
they talk to us as if we are asking for something that we don't
deserve but I don't care. I will continue to fight for her right to
a good education even if it's costing me a lot of time and money.

I am also trying to get some programs at the community club
for kids that don't play hockey or ringette. There are no other
programs there except skating and hockey. I'll see if I can get a
pre-school started so that Sunita can go when she is old enough.
I am finding out that raising kids is not easy and it's expensive.
My dream of owning my own business has finally happened. I
bought a small salon which I operate by myself on shorter than
normal business days of each week. I thought it was a good

idea at the time but I am now juggling two kids and a business because Robin is still working long hours.

1981

Dear diary,

I have neglected you for a long time but life is even more hectic now that I have a third daughter, Subhadra Samantha. Robin wanted a son but that was not to be. I can't really understand that thinking so I asked him why a son was so important. He said that all Indian men want to have a son or many sons and he wanted someone to carry on his name. I used to hear mom tell me that before I was born, most men wanted to have sons but Daddy wanted to have a daughter first and he was very happy when I was born. On the day I was born, Nani told mommy that she should name me Savitree but mommy said that her boss Mr. Kawall already had a daughter named Savitree so he would think that she was copying the name. Then daddy came home from selling milk and when Nani told him that he had a daughter, he dropped his milk cans and ran up the stairs to see me. Then he decided that he would name me Savitree but Mommy gave him the same reason that she gave Nani. Mom told him to go to a pandit and get my name from the Patra because it was important that the name be the right one. The pandit opened the Patra and said that they should name me Savitree. So it looks like my name was destined to be Savitree.

I didn't do that for my daughters because I am not even sure if there is a pandit in Winnipeg and besides, I am Christian I think. I have not gone to church since before I left Guyana. Church became about dressing up and not about praying so I stopped going. Robin is Hindu but he doesn't really practice. We picked Hindi names but not because of his religion but because those are names that we like. I often think that the kids should go to Sunday school or have some religious practice but I myself don't want to go to church. Does that make me a hypocrite wanting them to know about God but not wanting to go myself? I don't want them to be influenced by my opinions or feelings about religion. I suppose all the shouting by the pastor of Redeemer church must have affected me in some way because sometimes I feel that God is going to punish me for not taking them to church. Then I tell myself that one of the reasons that I stopped going to church was that I would not believe that if God is a great God, he would punish us. We are told that men and women marry each other because they love each other and although I did not marry for that reason, God would not be vengeful. I think I am trying to make myself feel better for not taking the kids to Sunday school.

Dear diary,

I had to sell my salon about a month ago because one of my clients told me that the woman I hired to run the salon while I was pregnant was stealing from me. I couldn't manage all of it so I am now back to cutting hair at home for some of my clients who don't want to go anywhere else. All those neighbours who I used to give free haircuts to wouldn't pay to come to the salon for the last two years but now that I am home again, they want free haircuts again. I realize now that my labour as a hairstylist is worth something to me so I am not doing that any more. I didn't feel bad about selling the business because it was a lot of work. I can now say that I had my own salon if only for two years. I know my in-laws were not happy about me becoming a hairstylist but now that I have my own business, they are telling people that I am a salon owner. I think they feel that being the owner of a salon had more status in society than just being a hairdresser.

With three kids to take care of, and Robin still working long hours, I have all the responsibility for taking care of the children. Several families including me got together and started a babysitting co-op. We modeled it after a co-op that one of the women belonged to in Florida. We have a formal structure with bylaws and we pay each other with points. Each point has a monetary value of 50 cents but we don't use actual money, only points. I am the bookkeeper/secretary and I get paid some points each month for managing the books. The president of the co-op also gets paid some points each month for planning and chairing meetings. It's a great system and we all know each other. New families are only accepted on a member's recommendation so we know our kids will be safe with the other parents who are babysitting. We are now up to fifteen families because everyone wants to join but we are sticking to our rules about how new families join. We had to refuse some families because they want babysitters but don't want to babysit in return. They don't really understand how a co-op works – that it is owned by members and everyone has to contribute to its success. I also have a membership at the Red River Co-op so we try to buy much of our groceries there and I look forward to the cheques I receive from them every year for shopping at those stores.

Some of the families use the co-op a lot so we are now discussing whether we should offer other services for points. The members know that I am a hairstylist so they would like to get haircuts if I would take points for the cuts. I think if the co-op members decide to offer services for points, we'll all benefit because I can offer haircuts, some people sew, some people can offer the produce they grow in their gardens and some people offer typing or carpentry services. I'll let you know what we decide.

With the three girls, I have a bigger car than the Chevette that we bought two years ago. This one is a Buick and it has nice velvet seats. We can afford a few more things nowadays but I am still very careful with my money, preferring to buy things for the kids rather than spending money on me. I've become a good money manager especially when it comes to preparing healthy meals on a small amount of money. I cook most things and I always pack a good lunch for Sharmi because she doesn't come home for lunch. All that financial work in Dad's trucking business is coming in handy now that I have a family.

1982

Dear diary,

Lots of changes happening. Robin left his job at Reid Crowther and is now working for the federal government. He is working in a more managerial role but the politics is rather overwhelming. There is a strong hierarchy of supervisors who like to let him know his place, meaning it is a less friendly work environment than the previous job. That will be something to get used to but his salary is much higher than he was making before.

Sunita started school in September and I am still battling with the school board. French Immersion parents are still paying bussing fees but we are fighting to get the fees dropped because there are different rules for bussing English and French Immersion students when they should all be entitled to free bussing. The cost is now $750 for the first child and $375 for each additional child. We are now paying more than $1000 a year just the get the kids to and from school. We found the money to do that but it's a tight budget. At least the school now has a library and we have enough French teachers to teach all the subjects in French except English classes. We are making progress but the superintendent must be annoyed every time he sees us because he knows that we'll ask for something else.

I think I am the only parent in the group who did not go to university or college so he usually treats them with more respect than he offers to me. I can feel it when he talks to me as if I am beneath him.

The other battle I am fighting is with the Manitoba Department of Labour. I have a few clients who are shut-ins so I go to their home to do their hair just like I used to when I was at Pollock's but it is illegal because people's homes are not salons as defined by labour legislation. I went to the office and talked to the person in charge of hairstylists to ask if they would consider changing the regulations to allow people like me to have a mobile business. She said that there are safety concerns for me. I said that plumbers come into my home and no one worries about their safety. She said that I would have to charge a lot for the services. I said that would be up to me not her to charge whatever fee I wanted for my service just like a plumber would do. She said there are health concerns. I said that she could issue licences and establish health standards. She said I was argumentative and dismissed me from her office saying that the matter was closed. None of those reasons make sense but it is another example of people in authority holding on to that authority even when they know that what they are saying is not logical. I didn't make the least bit of headway but I'll keep trying. I don't give up that easy.

1985

Dear diary,

My life is getting more hectic with each passing year. This year, we took the three girls back to Guyana for their first international vacation – well, except for the US. We saved hard to do this but it was important for me to take them because I want them to know their heritage and when I talk about growing up in Belair, they'll know what I mean. They had a great time but I prepped them before we left Winnipeg about how poor some people are including some of my family and told them they are not to ask for anything to eat or drink. That was my attempt to save my family members over there any embarrassment. I even took a suitcase full of food like cold cereal, canned fish and canned milk so that the kids would have things to eat because much of the food stuff over there is now contraband and people can be imprisoned for being caught with certain foods like the ones we were taking. We were allowed to take the food because we were foreigners but if we were caught selling any of it, we'd be in trouble too.

I need not have worried about my kids not wanting to eat the local food. They ate roti and vegetables for breakfast just like everyone else over there and we gave our families the things we brought. They loved having the contraband items and my kids were just as happy to eat the local food, some of which they are used to eating because I try to shop at some Chinese super-markets in Winnipeg which have tropical fruits and vegetables, albeit expensive. The kids were so good. They blended in with everyone over there and wanted to do any and everything. We visited many family members all through the east coast all the way to Golden Fleece. They played with Auntie Bhano's chickens, flew kites at Easter and just really enjoyed every aspect of their time in Guyana. At one point toward the end of the vacation, Sunita and Sharm asked where all my poor relatives lived. We had visited some but the kids were totally oblivious to who was poor and who was rich. They thought that running around someone's yard picking and eating fruits and chasing down chickens and trying to make them swim in a barrel of water was pure fun. What they didn't know, as I didn't when I was a child, was that the fruits they were happily picking and eating were sources of income that my aunt and cousins sold at the market each week. Same for the chickens. And the water they were putting the chicks and ducklings to swim in was drinking water for the family - collected in barrels and stored for use so putting the chicks to swim was not good. Of course they learned from my cousin who saved a drowning chick that chickens do not swim and losing a young chick means losing a source of income and chickens over there were not really pets.

Life has changed so drastically for Guyanese people. Many of them are now dependent on family living abroad and more and more they have become less and less self-sufficient. Many Indian families are leaving the country as fast as they can get out. It seems each year I am watching my beloved country of birth descend into something I don't even know any more. The buildings in Georgetown which used to be considered the pride of the Caribbean have become so run-down and dinghy. I had to go to a hospital for an x-ray for an injury I got when I fell and because my uncle had some connections and another uncle was a doctor, I was able to bypass a long line of people sitting on the floor waiting to get an x-ray. I walked past as if I did not notice because my shoulder was in agony but months later, I felt the sting of guilt that my privilege allowed me to do that. Some of them may have been in as much pain as I was but I didn't care to notice at the time. I can still see the eyes of some of the people who were sitting there – some of them for hours before the office opened. Mom said it was like that in the old days but it was much worse now – only I never experienced it then and I didn't a few months ago.

Diary, it's funny how quickly I went back to accepting the privileges I used to have when I was so resentful of not having any when I arrived in Canada. I wanted my children to learn something about my country of birth but the one who learned a few important lessons was me. In my effort to survive in Canada, I had forgotten how much I used to help people when I was a child.

1986

Dear diary,

You are such a faithful friend even when I neglect you for years. It's not that I want to. It's just that I am so busy with the kids and working part-time that I can hardly keep up with everything I want to do. Subhadra is now in kindergarten and she is in French Immersion. Look how far we have come diary. By the time Sunita started French Immersion kindergarten in 1982, the school board relented and we paid full bussing fees for the first child and half as much for the second child. That's still more than $1000.00 per year just to get them to school and home but it'll be worth it. The kids are doing well at school and they are learning about Manitoba's French Canadian culture and about how the Voyageurs contributed to Manitoba. I am happy about that because they are Canadians and they should know their country's history.

The only time I was not pleased about school had nothing to do with French. Sunita is a very sociable child and one day she came home and told me that her teacher hit her with a ruler on her knuckles. I went crazy because I had memories of my own childhood when the teachers used to flog us for no good reason. I went to the school and told the teacher that if she ever hit Sunita again, I would report her to the school board office. She didn't do it again but I am nervous that it could happen again and I won't be able to protect her. I don't want those horrors repeated on my kids. By the time Subhadra started kindergarten this year, the school board dropped the bussing fee so it's now free. Yeah diary. We would have found the money to pay for her too but there are a lot of parents who can now make French Immersion a choice if they want to. Some of the English parents think we should be paying the bussing fee because we are rich – I mean that French Immersion parents are rich – but I know we're not rich. We made a choice about the girls' education and we had to pay for that choice. Anyway, that's one battle won but there are so many more to fight.

We moved into a new house in July and I do miss having the community centre across the street but this new street is now much quieter. I am proud of myself for the work I did at the club in Waverley Heights. When I lived there, I went over and asked for programs for kids who did not play hockey or ringette. The board said it was a lot of volunteer effort to offer such programs so I joined the community club executive and helped to plan for some programs that did not include hockey. There is now a nursery school and dance classes and we had carnivals in the summer so the kids could feel that the centre is more than hockey and skating. We held dances on New Year's Eve, Halloween and summer for the adults so it's now a real community. We even opened a canteen for the kids and parents.

I am proud of the work and I know even though I am now in a new community, the other one will continue. We are the second family to move into Whyte Ridge so it will take some time to start a new community club. I now have to contend with limited bus service and no grocery stores in the neighbourhood. Before we moved we asked about those services and the builder said the city is planning to start a bus route but so far, there is nothing. I don't have to worry yet because the kids are still being bussed to school but I can see them stopping Sharm's bus soon. I called someone at the transit office and he said that the city is considering limited bus service in the morning and afternoon for two hours. The taxes are one of the highest in the city and there is very little service for what we are paying. Hmmm, we should have spent some more time thinking about all of that before we decided to move here but the other house was getting too small for all of us. We are now considered upper middle class by some of our friends - whatever that means - because we've moved into a new and big house. Up till now, I have not thought of that but I suppose that living in a new house with a two-car garage and two living rooms makes people think we are rich. If I think of where I started in Canada, living with my in-laws for two years in a basement bedroom, this is a huge change in 16 years but it has been with a great deal of hard work and sacrifices for both Robin and I.

We were fortunate when we bought the first house on Waller for such a good price so when we sold it only three years later for double the purchase price, we had enough money to only have a small mortgage on the next house. Before we sold that one, we planned carefully and figured out how much we could afford for a mortgage and still have enough money for the kids to go to school and pay for after school activities. We finally decided to get the house custom built by Arborlea Homes and that way, we could decide what we could leave for later. Robin is good at the engineering part so he figured out what foundation things we could put in place so that we could add to them later. I want a sunroom when we can afford it but for now all we can afford is the piles for the sunroom. That's okay because I have a vision for what I want and I can wait for it. We paid $100,000 and borrowed the additional $60,000 from Belgian Credit Union. I found out that credit unions work on a similar principle as a co-op – that it is member- owned so the mortgage rates are slightly less and we can repay on the principal without the same penalties as the big banks. We estimate that it might take us about ten or more years to pay off the mortgage.

Subhadra is in kindergarten so I am planning for when she is in school full-time. Since there are few people who live in this neighbourhood, it is difficult to find a babysitter so I am considering building a salon in the basement. This way, I won't have to worry about finding a sitter for those in-service days but I have no idea how or where I will get clients since there are hardly people living around us. I could advertise for clients but it would be too far for people in Fort Garry to travel. Then

I have to think of a zoning variance and hope that the city will grant it. Since there are few neighbours around, no one might object to my having a salon in my home. Maybe next year. In the meantime, I started working part-time at a salon on Kenaston but it is very few hours a week. My plan is to build a clientele of a few people who may be willing to come to my home if I build the salon.

1988

Dear diary,

The years are passing too quickly and I have less and less time to write. We finally have bus service in the neighbour-hood but it's only for two hours in the morning and afternoon. It's better than nothing but still bad. I still keep writing to the Department of Labour about getting a mobile licence. I am still going to people's homes and I know it's not legal but I feel sorry for those people. Some of them have arthritis and can hardly walk, some have strokes, three are agoraphobic and one is in a wheelchair. The government has to recognize that people need these services and it's not a luxury but no one seems to be listening. Some days I am frustrated but not enough to want to stop. Dad keeps telling me I can't save the world. Maybe I am only trying to save myself or my soul, not the whole world. I don't like people taking advantage of others especially when they are in a position to know and do better. I joined the Whyte Ridge Residents Association and we are trying to petition the city to get better bussing and to get a community club built here but that is going to be a long battle again. We are planning some community activities so that people can get to know each other. It feels like I am doing the same thing like I did in Waverley Heights only 12 years later.

The committee meets at South Winnipeg Technical Centre which is a new trade school that was built four years ago. Finally, a trade school in the south end of the city. I remember back in high school when I told the school counsellor that I wanted to be a hairdresser and she told me that I had to leave Massey and go to another school outside the division. Diary, let me tell you about the centre. I received an invitation to the sod-turning ceremony from Lloyd Axworthy who is the federal Member of Parliament for this district so maybe that's why the school is here. I don't know why we received one but I was glad to go. I had to drive over a dirt road – well not a road exactly – a snow track which led to a tent where the sod was being turned. There was nothing around and I mean nothing except some bushes. The school is a unique partnership between the Fort Garry School Division, the St. Vital School Division and the Assiniboine South School Division but I was curious as to why they would build a school in what was then a field. I guess they knew the development plans for the area because here we are two years later, living in this new community of Whyte Ridge. The school is not built in the community though. It's standing alone in a field surrounded with light industrial businesses. I feel a kinship with the centre maybe because they have a hairstyling program or maybe it is the hope for students who choose not go to university. Whatever the reason, I want it to succeed as though I have some personal stake in it.

It's now two years since we are in this house and I did open my little salon in the basement last year. I have some clients and I hope to grow the business some more. I love doing hair and having the salon at home means I can take appointments when the kids are in school and can be free when they come home so I can take them to their after school activities and I can still contribute financially to our family. The added bonus is that I am getting to meet people in the neighbourhood. The kids are involved in swim lessons and also in their church activities.

Yes, diary, I said church. I didn't tell you about it because I was embarrassed to share that with you. When we were living in Waverley Heights, some church people came to our house and asked if we wanted to join the Baptist church which was having services at the junior high across the street from our house. I told them that I was not interested in going to church but wanted my children to go and experience God so they came to pick up the kids each week for Sunday school. The Baptist church now has its own building on Waverley Street so the kids are going to Sunday school and one weeknight activity there. I feel better about the kids going to church but I still feel like a hypocrite. I know you have never judged me but it's my own guilt that made me keep this from you.

Dear diary,

I considered opening a salon in the new strip mall in Whyte Ridge but the landlord and I could not agree on a space. I wanted a small space and the landlord agreed but changed his mind because he wanted me to rent a larger space. I was worried I would not have enough clients to pay the bills so I decided not to take the space. I was so disappointed because I really want to open a big spa salon like I had envisioned in my head. I spoke to Pam about it. She is a client I had at Kenaston Hairstyling and when I started to work from home, she came here with me. She is quite smart, works at Red River Community College and is one of the few clients who doesn't think that all hairdressers are simpletons. Yes diary, over the years, I have had clients who seemed surprised that I could discuss topics such as world politics, geography or education with any degree of competence. I really like her and we have some great conversations about all kinds of topics. She has a master's degree and she often tells me about the work she does at Red River. It sounds very important and I am proud to say that I can converse with her about some of the things she tells me.

Diary I remember how she laughed at the story I told her about the client who came into the Kenaston salon and didn't want me to cut her hair because I was coloured. I was standing several feet from that client when she said that and of course my face turned red. Sybil, the owner was quite angry and told her to leave. Sybil is Jewish and afterward she told me she had enough of people judging her because she is Jewish so she is not going to allow the client to do the same to me. I felt so good that someone stood up for me like that. It's embarrassing to hear someone say that about me for no good reason. Many salon owners are not fair to their employees but not Sybil. When it's not busy, other owners send the stylists home without pay and if they complain, they get fired. It's awful but the stylists don't complain because they can't afford to lose their jobs. They come to work each day but sometimes go home with only two or three hours pay. Erica and Sylvia never did that to me and neither did Sybil. Maybe I am one of the lucky ones to have had good employers. The same client let me cut her hair but she kept telling me how she lived in Singapore for a year and she had a servant who looked just like me. She asked about my husband and when I said he was an engineer, she asked which train he drives. I said he is a mechanical engineer and got his degree from the University of Manitoba. I could see that she looked like she did not believe a word I was saying. Each week for several weeks she would come in and tell me the same story as if to make sure I knew my place as a hairdresser and as a coloured person. I told Robin each week about her veiled insults. He enquired about her husband's name and told me that he knew the client's husband. In fact Robin was an expert witness against the company my client's husband worked for in a matter related to income tax charges. I told this to my client after several more weeks of insults and that finally shut her up. Patience is a virtue that I am learning to cultivate but it's hard.

Dear diary,

I am so excited that I could not get to you fast enough to share my big news! Remember when I was telling Pam how disappointed I was that my plans for opening a salon were not going to happen? I was moaning about how I didn't know what I was going to do with my life and I seemed to be losing some focus so she came up with this crazy idea. She suggested that I go to Red River Community College to become a vocational teacher. That was the craziest thing I ever heard. Me a teacher? What would I teach? Isn't that crazy? I told her exactly that. She explained that as a vocational teacher I could teach hairstyling but that was all I would be able to teach. That shut me up right away. I was had never considered teaching, let alone teaching something I love. The idea was quite overwhelming. You know how I can talk but you know how when someone says something that is kind of life changing, it makes me quiet? Well this was one of those crazy ideas. I have never ever thought about teaching – ever. Besides, I said that I didn't feel smart enough to be any kind of teacher even if it was to teach hairstyling. She said to sleep on it then go and talk to Jim McKay at the teacher education office and tell him that she sent me to enquire about the vocational teacher education program.

I'm not sure if I slept on it. It felt more like I stayed awake for an entire two weeks thinking about it and finally built up enough courage to go to see Jim McKay. He was very nice and talked to me about half an hour about the full-time and the part-time program. My heart was pounding so hard I thought he must surely have heard it. He gently asked me when I could enrol in the part-time teacher education program and said that if I started right away, he could give me the first course package to take home with me. Well guess what, diary? I DID!! I am totally nervous about it but I can't stop thinking about teaching something I love to do and I grinned all the way home. I am doing the *Introduction to Instruction* course by correspondence and I really like it. Jim said that I can apply to the full-time program which starts next September and I will be able to get credit for the courses I finish this year. I never imagined that I would be a teacher but I am excited. The kids are all in school full-time and I can now dedicate some time to studying. Is this really my life? I am not a teacher yet but I am already planning that if I am lucky, I might be able to get a job at South Winnipeg Technical Centre. Wouldn't that be great? Me as a teacher? I keep saying the words over and over trying to imagine myself in that role.

1989

Dear diary,

I applied to the full-time vocational teacher education program and I was accepted this fall. I had to do an interview with a hairdressing teacher and Jim McKay. He was very nice but the other person was not quite so nice. She asked some questions related to perms and colours and Jim focused on the questions about why I want to be a teacher. I was nervous but afterwards, he said I did well in the interview. There are 12 of us in the program and three of us are hairstylists. I received credits for the three courses I have already taken since last fall and this summer so I don't have as busy a schedule as the other students.

One of the courses was Introduction to computers and I bought myself a Tandy computer to learn how to use it. I am even learning how to type which is much nicer than typing on a typewriter but I am still not good at it. I think I have a mental block when it comes to typing because it reminds me so much of the old days of typing long invoices only to make one mistake at the end and then make a mess trying to correct the carbon copy and have to start the whole invoice all over again.

I have been spending a lot of time volunteering on the parent council at Viscount Alexander, Pembina Crest and Vincent Massey. Sharm is now in high school and still in the French Immersion program. With the three girls in three different schools it's quite a juggle to help out at each one and still have time to do the household chores and find time to study. I am doing quite well in school and I'm thoroughly enjoying studying. It sounds strange to say that especially when I think back of how much time I spent skylarking at Cumming's Lodge school. I feel like I've found some new best friend in my books.

Diary, I forget to mention that we bought another house. It's a three bedroom townhouse that we are going to rent out. Robin and I talked about it and we think that buying it may mean we take longer to pay off our mortgage but this would be a good investment. Imagine me becoming a landlord. I am not going to be the kind of bad landlord I hear about. We are renting the house to four university students who are sharing the rent. They are good tenants but the rent is not always on time. I feel bad for them so we remind them after a few days and they usually pay up. I don't like being a landlord but I think that when the kids are older, we'll sell the house and use the money to pay for their university or college.

1990

Dear diary,

It's the beginning of the new year and so much has happened. You won't believe this but I got a job as a teaching assistant at South Winnipeg Technical Centre starting this month. I finished my first semester of the vocational teacher education program and I am more than halfway done with all my courses. Two teachers in the teacher education program don't appear to be too motivated to teach. I ask a lot of questions and I can see they are irritated with me but I don't care. One of them often doesn't even make the effort to come to class. If we want to show him our assignment, we have to go to the cafeteria to see him. We end up teaching each other and a few students even handed in the same assignment on different days to him and he didn't notice. He expected all of our assignments to be handed in by the end of October even though the course outline says we have until early December to hand them in. I heard from other students that he wants us to hand in our work early so he can have the rest of the semester off so I decided to be contrary and not hand mine in until the last day. He saw me in the cafeteria several times and reminded me I had not submitted all my assignments. I told him I would have them ready by the due date. I had actually finished them and I really didn't need to be in the cafeteria because I brought my lunch every day but I wanted him to see me and ask so that I could say no. I know that wasn't nice but I am so hungry to learn that I think if he is the teacher, he should be expecting more from us not less and certainly he should be giving more of himself.

Mr. Starsiak is the toughest teacher but he is the one I learned the most from. I did the computer course with Jim McKay and I also learned a lot from him but in the beginning when I asked him questions about the software, he would fix it but I asked him to show me how to do it for myself otherwise I won't learn. One of my classmates in that class asked me to print my computer assignments and he turned them in as his work but I don't know how to tell him that I didn't want to do that. I know it's cheating and I should have said something but I didn't. Now I wish I had because he is teaching at South Winnipeg Technical Centre where I am now working. I wonder what he tells his students about cheating.

I used to do to poor Mr. Pollock the same thing that I did to Jim. I would pester him to teach me what he knew. He used to keep the client cards with the formulae in a file behind the main desk and when a client wanted a colour, he would mix it and we would apply it and at the end of the processing time, he would check the colour and decide when it should be washed off. I was not learning anything about mixing colours so I started following him around when he was mixing the colours and each day I would ask 1001 questions about why he was doing what he was doing. When I asked why he kept the client cards at the desk and wouldn't allow the students to mix the formula, he said that it was to prevent mistakes but I think it was to make sure the clients didn't copy the formula and go to another school. It was a way to keep his customers coming back to him. I was so persistently annoying that he finally relented and started teaching me about working with chemicals on different types of hair textures. He was a superb colourist and I learned a lot from him. That's why I think I am a good hairstylist when it comes to creating and correcting hair colours.

We took the kids to England and Europe for a nice vacation. It was a bit expensive but I have become very efficient at money management so in spite of building our house four years ago, we managed to set aside some money over the last couple of years to take a trip like this. We debated whether we should make a down payment on our mortgage but we felt it was important for the kids to experience the world through travel. I know most people cannot afford this opportunity but it's an important part of my children's education. I have denied myself things that I would like to have so they can have the things they need and the things we think are important to their educational growth. Of course they occasionally remind us of all their friends who have much more than they do but I also remind them that I volunteer at almost all their school activities and they always have home cooked meals and good lunches. Try that reasoning sometime with a child who sees her friends getting things she doesn't have and it goes over just like you would think it would – comparing an annual vacation to Mexico with slices of banana loaf or a meaty piece of lasagna in your lunch kit. Not an equitable comparison but Robin and I can't compete with that.

Dear diary,

This year is racing by. I have been doing exceptionally well at school – getting A's in all my courses. I am a dedicated student and I want to learn as much as possible but the more I learn, the less I feel I know. Sometimes I feel smart and other times I feel I am not quite getting what the teachers are saying. I want to contradict them when they talk about third world countries and give false information but I remain quiet because after all, they are the teachers and they must know. My confidence is not always as evident as people seem to give me credit for or at the very least, I don't always feel as confident around teachers who are supposed to know more than I do. When the information is wrong, why don't I say something? It may be a throwback to the days when I challenged my teachers and they either flogged me or punished my with bad grades. I love school and I love the time I spend volunteering at the kids' schools.

I was lucky to get the teaching assistant position at South Winnipeg Technical Centre. I was so excited to go to work but my first day on the job did not go well at all. I came home and had a good cry because all day at work my throat was hurting from wanting to cry but holding it in. I was standing next to two students and one of them said he needed some help with the hairstyle he was trying to create. The other student told him to ask me since I was the teaching assistant. He looked straight at me and announced he was not going to ask any Paki woman to help him. I couldn't believe what I was hearing. I stood there transfixed and not a single word would come out of my mouth. My face turned red from embarrassment because he said it so loud that several students looked up from their work. I could see as I watched them that they were shocked that he would make such a racist comment but I may have been the most shocked because it was directed at me. No one said a word, including me.

A few days later, the same student came up to me and asked for some help with his hairstyle as if he had not said something so cruel only a few days before. I had spent so much time with those comments in my head for days that I thought about all the things I would say to the student if he ever spoke to me. But in every scenario, I did not think about the response I eventually gave when the occasion arose. I asked him to confirm that he needed help and reminded him about what he said a few days before. He looked very uncomfortable but apologized about the remark. I told him that I was not from Pakistan and calling someone a Paki was a racial slur. He then said something very unexpected. He explained that he was Italian and as long as he could remember growing up, kids would call him by racial slurs so he thought that if he ever had the opportunity to do the same, he would do it. I asked him how he felt when other students called him names and I said I felt the same way when he did that to me. After that, we had a good relationship especially when he found out that my in-laws who lived down the street from him were often kind to him.

Dear diary,

I am once again lucky to be working at SWTC for such a good principal like Maxine. Many instructors don't have good things to say about her but after sitting in the staff room and listening to their discussions, more and more I am learning that the ones who are most upset are the ones who have the reputation for being slackers. She expects them to work hard and be account-able and she is not afraid to say that. They call her the *b" name but it doesn't seem to me that she has asked for anything out of the ordinary.

She had all my fees waived at Red River so the tuition for my part-time teacher education courses are paid by the centre.

That's like scholarship money. She also pays me as a teacher rather than a teaching assistant so I am doubly lucky. I asked her why she would do that. She said if I wanted to be paid as a teaching assistant she could oblige but I should not look a gift horse in the mouth or something like that. I had no idea what that meant but it sounded like she was telling me that she was doing something nice for me and I should accept it. She said I was a hard worker and someday soon I would be a good teacher. I am indeed fortunate to have had the guidance of several good women in my life since coming to Canada because women are not generally in positions of authority. I only hope that someday I will be able to do the same for someone else.

Oh diary, I don't think I mentioned this but we bought another revenue house. It is in the same building as the other one but at the other end. There are four units in the building and we now own the larger two with three bedrooms each. That was a bit of a stretch for our budget but I think this is it for revenue homes. We have to start thinking of university tuition because in another 18 months, Sharm will be starting university. I've always assumed and planned and that the kids will go to university but I've never had the desire to go myself. I'm not planning to pursue that path even now that I know that it is possible because the vocational teacher education program at Red River has an articulation agreement with the University of Manitoba. I can see that going to university after high school would not have been the best choice for me. After all this time, I still love being creative and I am very happy to be teaching something I love to do.

1957-Top-Dood; Front - L to R: Sandra, Sharie, Karran, Sabena

1961- L to R: Sandra, Sabena, Karran

1963: R to L: Sabena, Sandra

1970: Sandra

1970: Robin and Sandra

1995 - L to R: Robin, Sharmila, Subhadra, Sandra, Sunita

2002 - L to R: Sharm, Trent, Sandra, Robin, Sunita, Mike, Subhadra

2006 - Sandra

2012 - Back Row - L to R: Darwin, Sophie, Trent, Mike, Ronin,
Sunita, Sabena, Sharm, Sabreena, Sandra, Robin
Front Row - L to R: Izabel, Subhadra, Sharie, Sahana

1991

Dear diary,

It's three years since I started my vocational teacher education program at Red River Community College and I am now a graduate with a perfect score of 4.0. I can hardly believe that I got an A or A+ in every course. I really love learning about teaching. Remember when I was doing computer programming all those years ago and it was so boring? Well the computer course I took with Jim was not boring at all. I am learning so much and Pam has been such a good friend. We talk about teaching and she said that she is not surprised at my success because she always thought I was smart. I just have to believe in myself. I got a half-time job at Sturgeon Creek Secondary School for the winter semester and I loved it. The principal said I did such a good job that the hairstyling students I was teaching registered for next year so he offered me a half-time position in the Fall, then the enrolment went up some more so he offered me full-time work. But you know what diary? I turned it down. Some of my friends thought I was crazy to turn down such an opportunity because there are not that many teaching jobs in the public schools for hairstylists and I may not get the opportunity again. Diary, I have a bigger vision for my life. I always seem to have a different vision for my life than everyone else thinks I should have so it's hard to convince anyone that it makes sense for me.

I got a scholarship from the Manitoba Teachers Society. It's not that much – only $1,200, but if I don't take it this year, I'll lose it, so after some discussion with Robin, I decided to go to university with a full course load and work part-time as a substitute teacher at South Winnipeg Technical Centre to earn some extra money. It's interesting how one of the teachers says she doesn't understand why I want to go to university because my vocational education certificate would be quite sufficient to work as a sub. She told me that since my husband works for enough money, I don't really need to work; I've never discussed Robin's salary so I asked how she came to that opinion. She said the way I was dressed and the neighbourhood I live in made her come to that conclusion. It reminded me of something that Dad used to tell us when we were growing up. It was a lesson he learned from his uncle that it didn't matter how much or how little money he had, he should always pay attention to his physical appearance because people will judge you accordingly. It seems superficial but people are often judged by the way they dress and the work they do. Those stereotypes are hard to change.

I found many of my previous clients who knew nothing about me assumed I was a poor immigrant who couldn't do better because I am a hairstylist. In fact, a few years ago, one of them asked me if my husband was a taxi driver. When I asked why she would say that, she said: "I thought all you people worked as cleaners or taxi drivers." I told her my husband was a professional engineer but I could tell she didn't believe me. Then there are those people who know the neighbourhood I now live in and will assume that I must be well-off and don't need to work. I can't figure out how they judge that but one of the teachers at SWTC said that I drive a nice car and I dress with clothes that look expensive. Maybe I have those symbols that people attribute to social status without me realizing. I suppose if I have to think about it, growing up, Dad and Mom always expected us to present ourselves in the best way and that meant dressing well, and speaking and walking with confidence, back straight, no slouching and using correct grammar. I'm also learning and practising how to look and sound confident but that's because I don't like being spoken down to and I read that if you speak with confidence, people are more apt to listen.

Back to my scholarship. I know that one day, the decision I made to go to university will pay off and everyone will see that it was the right decision, but right now it's hard to think that way when I am giving up almost $50,000 a year and a some-what permanent job for a $1,200 scholarship. I am only saying this to you diary but secretly I am glad to be going to university because I actually never thought I would ever go through those doors. Of course I don't know if I will graduate but I am going to work hard and if I do, I could transfer all my Red River courses to the teacher education program at the University of Manitoba. I will try to finish my courses in two or three years so I can graduate with a Bachelor of Education by my fortieth birthday. That's hardly believable – me in university.

Robin and my parents are happy because they can see how much I still love hairdressing and how much I love being at school. I love the smell of the library and sometimes I just want to be left alone to read and study as much as I want to but that's not practical. I still have my salon business at home and the kids still need to eat and of course now that Catherine has passed away and Tiffany and Jarrod are living with us, it makes for a crazy life. When I told Catherine I would be the guardians of her children if anything ever happened to her, she wasn't sick and I didn't expect that my best friend would be dead at 39 and I would have to take care of her children as well as my own. I don't expect that Jarrod will be with us for too long because his dad is making him promises of a better life and I am not sure we can compete with that, nor do I want to. I now have five kids in five different schools and I am barely keeping my head above water. My studies offer a good respite from the madness that is now my life. I want to do the best for all five kids but some days it's all I can do to get through the day and keep my sanity. Sharm is now driving so that helps tremendously with getting everyone to and from school and you should see the kitchen at dinner and after when there are seven lunches to pack for the next day. Diary, this is a life lesson for me. I loved Catherine very much but I should have thought more carefully about what it would mean to really be the guardian of her children if she passed away. In this case I had less than one week from the time she got sick to the time she passed away. I want to keep my promise to her but it is a struggle to adjust to all these changes with no time to grieve the loss of my very best friend and confidante.

1992

Dear diary,

I have now completed my third year at university and I am doing very well. I took a cross-cultural education course with Fred Drew and it was as if I came alive. He is so knowledgeable about so many of the issues and challenges concerning cross-cultural and anti-racist education. I wish I knew as much as he does. I loved Dr. Bruno-Jofre's course the best. That was my first course ever at university and I was so nervous on the first day that all I wanted was to live through the day and not be noticed by her. Diary, what happened? I got to class just as it was about to start and there were only seats left in the front row so I had to sit right in front of her. I felt she was staring at me and I was sure she was asking herself why such an old student was in a first-year course. I sat quietly trying not to get noticed and would not respond to a single thing she asked. By the end of the class, she gave us an article by Henry Giroux and I had to read practically the whole article with a dictionary because there were so many words that were completely new to me.

At the start of the next class, I made sure to get there early so I could sit in the back row and hopefully hide from her. She asked if anyone read the article and a few hands went up including mine. What can I say? I am told to read so I do. She asked if one of us could say what the reading was about. I kept quiet. So did everyone else. Then she looked straight at me way at the back of the room and said: "Young lady, what about you? Can you tell me what you understood from the article?" I looked back to see if there was someone behind me who she might be looking at, but I was in the last row so there was no one else to answer but me. My face turned red as it usually does when I am embarrassed and I started explaining what I understood. She stared at me for the duration which felt like three hours but may have only been three minutes. I felt like I was speaking gibberish but apparently she didn't think so because when I was done, she clapped her hand and said the way I explained the article was precisely correct. I don't really remember what I said. Thirty-eight pairs of eyes were staring at me and I felt I was on a huge stage with my skirt stuck in my underwear. Ha!!!! At the end of class that day, I remember her telling me I should go to graduate school because I had a bright future.

I was so scared just being at university that it will be sufficient to get through the week and maybe the semester but graduate school is for really smart people and I will be satisfied if I could aspire to a bachelor's degree. Even though I earned my vocational diploma with a perfect grade point average, I feel that I lack the self-confidence so I constantly question my ability. I think a graduate degree may be beyond my ability. Mike Czuboka was another professor who was particularly complimentary and supportive. He said that as a teacher he never gives students anything over 90% even if they are very good because he thinks every student can aspire to something higher. When he said that one student's work was so outstanding that he broke his own rule, giving the student 95%, I looked around to see if I could tell who the student was. When I got my paper, I realized it was me. It's hard to explain how much I love learning. I earned all A's in the courses I took so far except for two English courses where I got a B+ and C+. I finally got over the fear of English from the days of Mr. Henderson and now it's payback time. I am majoring in English and even if I don't get all A's, and he'll never know or care whether I graduated or not, it's a boost to my self-confidence to realize that my academic ability has nothing to do with speaking English with a different accent. My days of being humiliated by my English teacher are over. It's as if my majoring in English is my way of proving to myself that I am capable academically. It's curious how teachers – good or bad – can affect you long after they have left your life.

Dear diary,

Things are less crazy in my life these days. Tiffany and Jarrod went to live with their dad – Jarrod a few months after coming to live with us and Tiffany by the end of last year - so it's been much less hectic, at least with only three kids to take care of. Sharm started university this year so my daughter and I are going to university at the same time. Fortunately for her, we're not in the same faculty and we don't travel together. Teenagers can feel embarrassed about being seen with their parents and I didn't want to put her in that position.

Do you remember last year when I was telling you I gave up a teaching job to go to school? Well I was subbing at South Winnipeg Technical Centre as a hairstyling teacher and they got a new director. He came into the classroom one day and we began to chat. He asked if I had any ideas about how the school could be better improved. I told him about the idea I had suggested to the administrators the year before about opening the school in the evenings, similar to what Mr. Pollock used to do for students who couldn't come to school during the day. Many of his students worked at dead-end jobs during the day and could not afford to quit those jobs to go to school so offering classes in the evenings would give many of them an opportunity to get the education they desired so they could earn a better living. I told him the administrators thought night school was a good idea but they offered several reasons why it would not be practical: 1) it would be too expensive; 2) no one would want to work all day and come to school full-time in the evenings; 3) the bus service was non-existent so students would have no way of getting home at night. I said we could do a survey but the suggestion went nowhere.

He said he would consider my suggestions as well as the reasons the administrators gave for not starting a night program. After several weeks he said he would start three evening programs in Hairstyling, Drafting and Industrial Electronics and he would like to offer me the hairstyling teacher's position if I wanted the job. I told him that when I made the suggestion of evening school, I was not suggesting that he hire me; I was only suggesting that if the facility is closed from late afternoon till the next morning, it might make sense to use the facility for evening programming for those who cannot come to school during the day, I certainly wasn't sure I wanted to work full-time, let alone in the evenings. I came home and talked to Robin and the kids and they thought it was a great opportunity I should not pass up. So I took the job and it allows me the flexibility to continue my studies in the daytime and work in the evenings. Hopefully I can manage the schedule of full-time work, full-time school, a home-based business and family commitments because it'll only be for another year and a half and I can graduate. I know that I am determined to do meet those commitments.

Dear diary,

I found out something interesting last night at work. When I accepted the teaching position, I was appointed lead instructor. That means I am the main point of contact at night if there is an emergency or some issue arises. I am also responsible for making sure the building is secure at the end of the night. The custodial staff are there to lock up and they are good at doing their work but I am the go-to person if any incidents arise.

Well this was the interesting part. I was speaking to an instructor who asked me if I get paid extra as a lead instructor. I said I get paid based on my qualifications and years of experience. He said that based on his role as a department head, I was doing the same work and more because I was the main contact person in the evenings if there were any issues. He said I should ask to be compensated at least as much as a department head was paid even though my title is Lead Instructor. He also suggested I speak to my union representative about this because I was being asked to perform more duties than a teacher. This was news to me. This is my first time working at a job where I am part of a union so I didn't even know I could ask them to represent me in what the instructor said was an unfair labour practice – giving me the title of lead instructor instead of department head even though I was doing more than a department head would do. I spoke to my union representative and he said there wasn't much the union could do for me because I was the only lead instructor in the college and it would hardly be worth negotiating for only one person. I asked him to compare my duties to that of a department head but he said my title was lead instructor, not department head. I asked if I might have been given a different title so I wouldn't have to be paid the same as a department head and he said it was possible but hardly worth pursuing.

Hmmm, my first encounter with my union has not gone so well. I remember in Guyana when the Trade Union Congress used to have posters around the country telling workers they had the right to strike if the working conditions were not good but it would hardly be effective for me to strike if my union isn't willing to support me. I thought unions were supposed to look out for the rights of their members but since there is only one of me, it doesn't seem to warrant the effort. I pay more than $900 per year for my membership so you'd think he would at least humour me and meet with the director even if I got nothing at the end. I would feel I had the support of my colleagues but I also know that several instructors are not happy about the college offering evening programs as they see it as a crazy idea that will fizzle out soon and is not worth the trouble everyone has to go through.

Diary, it is no trouble to any of the staff because none of the day staff were asked to work evenings. Every evening staff member is new to SWTC and working in the evenings is not exactly glamorous or easy work. We have no bus service, no student supports, no food service except for vending machines and no resource assistance for students. At the end of the night, students have to walk at least 10 minutes to catch the only available bus and then wait for another 20 minutes for it to arrive at the stop. I have been lobbying the college to provide food services for dinner because we cannot expect adult students who are working all day to come to school at night with no place to buy some dinner if they choose to. We asked for a few microwaves to be installed in the cafeteria so that those who bring their dinner can heat it up. I have even taken to bringing an extra meal every day for any student who may have forgotten their dinner. I know in some cases, some of them have no dinner to bring or money to buy something from the vending machine so they know I always have an extra one or I can ask one of the kids to bring an extra one from home since we live about two minutes from the college. The evening instructors provide the necessary remedial supports for the students who need academic help. We try to arrange for rides to the bus stop at nights and I even have a set of booster cables I keep in my classroom in case someone needs them. The students and teachers at night have become like a close-knit family – starting out of necessity and now, surprisingly, turning into looking out for each other.

So the day instructors have no reason to be resentful or upset about the evening programs. When asked, none of them would trade their day jobs for the evening job so I don't really understand why they are upset. I don't know for sure but I did hear from the instructor who first told me to talk to the union that the union representatives want the support of the rest of the membership so they have to tread a fine line. This is less clear to me. I did hear some talk that next year department heads will be reclassified as lead instructors. I'll wait to see if the union will do anything when the day instructors are involved.

Dear diary,

School is closed for the Christmas holidays and it's been a great term. I can't believe how much I have to learn about teaching. My courses at the university are coming in very handy to apply the learning though. I've been doing well so far, getting all As, even in my English classes. Just before school closed, the three evening teachers – me included – decided to host a potluck dinner for the evening students. We told the students that we (teachers) would provide the turkey, stuffing and gravy as well as the punch and coffee and they could bring whatever they wanted to contribute but did not have to feel obligated to bring something if it was not convenient. I knew it might be a financial struggle for some of my students but you know what? Every student in every class brought something. The culinary teachers offered to cook and carve the turkey for us and a few day staff who see the evening students on occasion helped us decorate the cafeteria with tablecloths, candles and table decorations.

There we were, like a huge family partaking in Christmas dinner even though some of the students are not Christian. No one seemed to care about religion. Some of the students even got dressed up for the occasion even though it was a regular class day and a few brought their families. We had not invited the families only because we would not have been able to accommodate everyone in the space. It was the most amazing sight to see. Students were clapping at all of our handiwork. At the end of the night there were huge amounts of food left over so we got some take-out containers from the food services department and we told the students they could help them-selves to any amount they wanted to take. All the food was taken and a few said they appreciated being able to take part in the dinner because it was the only Christmas dinner they were going to have. In Guyana people are poor but in Canada poverty is defined differently. When there is so much wealth over here, it is hard for me to imagine that someone in Canada would not have enough food.

Dear diary,

Robin's department amalgamated with another department last year. He and another colleague used to work hard, including a lot of overtime. They had to contend with one supervisor in particular who bullied them and used threats of firing if they didn't co-operate. Robin and his colleague concluded that they were targeted since they were not part of the supervisor's elitist group of friends. Robin keeps comparing his present bosses to his former supervisor Dave, who he says is the best boss he ever had. The new department is better, however, his new supervisor has his own group favourites and Robin and his colleague are not part of the in-group. The working situation is difficult because a staff member who reports to Robin often undermines his authority but there is no recourse because the employee is part of that inner circle of preferred people.

1993

Dear diary,

I really love teaching hairstyling. I have a very large class but the students are keen to learn. I teach by Individualized Competency-Based Learning. We prepare learning activity packages that students work through on their own. Most students don't have a problem but it's not the way that they are familiar with school (me neither) so some of them don't know how to use the packages. I should spend some more time teaching them how to use the packages rather than assuming they can do it on their own. But with a continuous intake of new students every month and such a large class of 24 students, it's hard to keep up with everything. The day teachers have only 15 students each but my numbers have always been from 18 to 20.

Do you remember when I used to volunteer at the hospital and I offered free haircuts to some of the patients who could not get out to a salon? Well I had this great idea when I started teaching last year that I could take my students to the hospital to offer hair and nail services to Geriatric patients. I thought it would benefit the patients and the students would have an opportunity to practice their skills. It took some planning but I pitched the idea to the director and he said I should talk to the administrators of the Victoria Hospital and if they support it and the students are agreeable, I could go ahead. I must have made a pretty convincing argument because everyone agreed it was a great idea so we now go every second week for three hours to the hospital. The students get to practice their hairstyling and communication skills and the clients benefit too by getting free haircuts or sets but more importantly, one of my reasons for doing this is that I wanted the students to learn about giving back to their community which benefits everyone– students, patients, hospital and South Winnipeg Tech. The students have to adjust their schedules to go there every second week at 12:30 pm but I don't penalize anyone if they can't go; most of them make the effort and will often arrange to leave work early or arrange for daycare so they can be at the hospital. Sometimes the clients give the students some tips so we combine the money and I add whatever else we need and we all go for a cup of coffee before our classroom is available for us at 3:45 pm. I am very happy and proud about how they are contributing and how much they are learning beyond hair skills and the effort they are making to do this.

Besides my teaching, I joined the Staff Development committee because I think SWTC should be making more of an effort to bring a cross-cultural dimension to the programs. Since I took the cross-cultural education course, I am seeing just how little we do at the centre. There are only adult students attending school in the evenings but the daytime is a combination of high school and adult students except for the hairstyling program which only has space for high school students, just because there are so many – especially girls – wanting to get into the program. The evening programs have large numbers of immigrant students, many who are very educated in their home country but cannot find work except for factory jobs so they are back at school trying to earn an education. I can totally identify with them. There are also a number of students who dropped out before completing high school and are now back for an education. We have to do more for these students but there is so much to do and so much I still don't know that at times it seems overwhelming to try to deal with all of it.

I have completed one more year of course work at the U of M so that's also keeping me pretty busy with studying. I've learned so much in the last few years about how education is political and it's making me become attentive to politics in a way I had not done before. I am still running my small business at home so Pam and I talk about education and how vocational education is seen as such a dumping ground for students who aren't doing well at academics. I am also learning from my experience as a student and as a parent that many teachers will work hard with their brightest students but will make less effort with those who need more help. I can see that at SWTC. The students feel they are part of a community and I can see how the evening teachers are dedicated to the success of their students. I think in some ways we're forced to care because other student supports are not there in the evenings. When I think back of the ways some of my teachers taught me, I consider myself lucky to have made it into university at all. Dr. Bruno-Jofre's course was most intriguing especially when we discussed Paulo Freire and Henri Giroux and their radical philosophy of education. I have to say that although most of my education so far has been traditional, I am favouring the radical philosophy. When I see my students being excited about volunteering, I know there can be a better world, but how to get there is the challenge.

Now here is an interesting piece of news. Remember last year when I told you about not getting compensated for my lead instructor responsibilities? Well this year the department head title was changed to lead instructor for all the day instructors and the union has now said that whatever the name change is changed to, lead instructors are department heads by another name and had to be compensated. So guess what? I am now getting a stipend for my extra evening duties. This is a union in action; one member's working conditions are not worth fighting for but four are. That's my little lesson but what is it? I want to think if my voice alone cannot be heard, my union representative would be my voice or stand beside me in solidarity. Disappointingly for me, that was not the case. Now I am getting a sense of what those signs that read "Solidarity Forever" meant when I was growing up in Guyana. I don't know the whole song but I do know the last line of the chorus was something about "the union makes us strong."

1994

Dear diary,

I gave myself a wonderful 40th birthday present – my graduation!!! I am very proud of myself. I finished my course work so that by my birthday on February 1st, I could say I achieved a feat that only a decade ago was not within my thoughts. I didn't think I would ever get through the doors let alone graduate. I attended my graduation and could hardly believe that at 40, I am a university graduate. When I used to go there with Robin in the early 70s to see Indian movies and attend engineering events, I used to think he was so smart to be going there and I would never be smart enough to be able to do that. I even majored in English and Vocational so after 22 years of feeling the sting of Mr. Henderson's awful treatment, I have finally put that to rest. I feel that my continued love for reading and writing and the validation from other professors have allowed me to let go of those feelings of inadequacy that he made me endure.

This is the best part, diary. Crazy as it is, not only did I graduate with a 3.7 GPA, I followed Dr. Bruno-Jofre's suggestion and applied and was accepted into the Masters of Education program. I have to admit I was a bit anxious about enrolling in further studies because I didn't know how Robin would feel.

Growing up in Guyana, girls are not expected to aspire to an education beyond high school and definitely they are not expected to have more education than their husbands, hence my concern. Robin was very supportive of doing my masters, and Dad and Mom were overjoyed. I am not the first in our family to go to university, Karran was, but I am the first to try at this level. Robin's mom was apprehensive because "people" might say I have more education than he does. Do people really care about that anymore? The kids were very supportive and thought I should do it if I want, so I did, diary. I did. I enrolled and started my program in May. I am going to continue to focus on adult and cross-cultural education within vocational education because I realize it's where my heart is. There aren't many women in vocational education at this level but that is not surprising because most of my classmates in the vocational courses were men. In several of the courses, I was the only woman but I am up for the next challenge. I am encouraging some of my female peers at South Winnipeg to complete their Bachelor's but not many are interested.

Dear diary,

Graduate school is very disappointing. I did my first course in Research Methods but it was a lot of proving and disproving hypotheses through statistics and analyzing variables using ANOVA and MANOVA or some such idiotic thing. I DO NOT like this course at all and the teacher is very boring. He talks as if we all understand everything he is saying but I feel completely lost. I am sure I am not the only one but everyone in class is nodding their heads when he says something so I do the same and of course I have no clue. When I do my assignments, it's evident because he wants one thing and I give him something else completely unrelated so he looks at me and I can tell he thinks I am dense. Well, I am when it comes to statistics. I considered calling Jim Ferguson but I'm even more afraid of logarithms even though I have no idea if it has anything to do with this course. I feel like a dunce but I have to pass this initial course to go on to the other courses.

Dear diary,

I passed my Research Methods course with a B+ but I had to work very hard for it. I am glad to be done but the professor said if I intend to do a PhD at a later time, I will need to do a research-based rather than a course-based masters and I will need to know the material in this course. I decided that since I won't be doing a PhD, I'll do the course-based masters and I will never have to do any research ever again.

Most of the courses at the graduate level are offered in the evenings because, of course, teachers with an undergraduate degree are teaching during the daytime. I am fortunate that the director at SWTC let me adjust my teaching schedule so I could do my prep work during the daytime and be off one evening a week when a substitute teacher comes in and takes over my class for a few hours. All teachers at the centre get one prep day in six and that day is covered by a regular substitute teacher. So instead of taking a full prep day in the evenings, I go in to work at 12:30 pm and finish at 6:30 pm and the sub takes over from 7pm -10pm so I can attend university classes. It is quite a juggle each week to arrange course work, clients, family obligations and my school work, but somehow I'm managing. It is a schedule beyond crazy but I want to learn so much that I feel like I am running out of time. I started school so late so I have to play catch-up although I am not sure who I am catching up to.

Some of the teachers at the school were not pleased I get to adjust my schedule so they complained to the director. He told them all they needed to do was ask and they could receive the same privileges of doing their prep work in the evening if they so wished. None of them so wished to spend their day at home and come to work in the evenings. Many of them have openly stated that they have no desire to go get a B.Ed and based on the number of years they have been teaching with a vocational teaching certificate, the evidence is there. Some of them have questioned why I want to further my education when it is not necessary if I teach hairstyling. They see acquiring a bachelor of education as a move up on the teachers' pay scale. For me, while the increased pay will be good, getting my B.Ed. is my effort to continue to learn to be a good teacher. Now that I have done so many other courses, I realize how much there is to learn about teaching beyond what I learned there. I hope that ultimately, my students will be the beneficiaries of my learning because I want to be the best teacher I can be. Anyway, the learning and studying are great; it's the other life events that are getting hard to manage.

1995

Dear diary,

I am pretty thrilled about the Victoria Hospital project, winning an award from the prestigious Conference Board of Canada for business/education partnerships. My students were pretty happy about their work being recognized nationally and it was exciting to see so many educational institutions partnering to do great work in their communities. I got to go to New Brunswick to receive the award and $1,000 which goes to South Winnipeg Tech. As great as that was, there was one downside just when I was about to leave for the event. I was given a layoff notice. I mentioned that the centre is a joint program with three school divisions but my program is entirely for adults.

I am under a collective agreement for public school teachers so if adult students do not register for their program of studies by the beginning of May, the school issues layoff notices according to the collective agreement. Most times adult students are still enrolling over the summer for Fall so rather than taking a risk that the programs will be full by the Fall, the centre issues layoff notices to all the evening instructors and some daytime instructors who also have adult students. It's very stressful to have a permanent teaching contract that isn't really permanent at all and I've faced this situation each year since I started teaching full-time. The union is not willing to take up the issue because there are so few of us affected that it doesn't seem to be worth the effort. Okay diary; explain to me how unions are supposed to work because I am still not getting it. After three years of paying close to $1,000 per year, I still have no support from the people who are supposed to be my voice. It's another hard lesson I had to learn. I've decided that maybe it's time for me to become a member of the union executive for our local. That may help me to have a better understanding of negotiations and bargaining.

I am making progress with my master's and I am learning a lot especially in the course on the Study of Teaching. I had to videotape and critique my teaching and interactions with students and that was a real eye opener. I have a student who wears a hearing aid and the tape made me see how I was doing him an injustice because I would often comment on his work as I was walking by but what I needed to do was stop by his station and talk to him because he relies on lip reading as well to hear what is being said to him. I had never thought of that before even though I did a course on special education in my undergraduate studies but that one focused more on students with behavioural issues.

Dear diary,

I am back at teaching. I received my recall notice from the centre at the end of July so I had a good rest over the summer after all. It was a busy time for us. Sunita graduated from high school but she decided she did not want to stay in Manitoba for university so she went to Calgary and she is staying with Bena and attending the U of Calgary. I was not ready to see her go but she insisted she did not want to go to U of M because there were too many people she'd rather not have to hang out with. I went to Catherine's plot at the cemetery because I felt I needed to talk to my best friend. That was the very first time since she passed away in 1991 that I went to her gravesite. I could not bring myself to let her memory go so I reasoned that if I did not go to her gravesite, then I could convince myself she had not really left me. Ours was such a close connection that I was sure she could read my thoughts and I could read hers. When our kids were toddlers, I used to drag her to the card stores and I'd stand and read and laugh at greeting cards which she thought was the silliest thing until she moved away to Calgary and found herself doing the same thing to feel close to me.

I miss her very much every day and I feel that I failed her in some way because I could not fulfil my promise to her to keep Tiffany and Jarrod safe. They went to live with their dad because he promised them the world but they have been living on their own for at least a couple of years. I am very disappointed with myself for not trying harder but at the time I didn't know what else to do. I was in a tough place – either fight through the courts to keep them with us when I had no legal right to keep them or let them go live with their dad and save my family and myself from the tragedy that we would ultimately face. It seemed that after Catherine passed away, my family was plunged into a chaotic situation; I had no time to grieve because it was hard enough keeping my sanity with the conflicting pressures of five children and my own studies. The emotional strain of dealing with her loss and suddenly having my family increase from five people to seven was becoming increasingly difficult for everyone and I felt if something didn't change, my entire family would fall apart as it was starting to from the pressures of dealing with loss and too many changes at once.

Dear diary,

It's now the middle of December and we are getting ready for the annual Christmas dinner for the evening students. Last week I had an appalling incident happen at school. Several years ago some students were gunned down at a polytechnic in Montreal and a group of men started a white ribbon campaign to draw attention to the issue of violence against women. A few years ago I decided I would do my part to draw attention to the issue so during the white ribbon campaign, I put up some posters around the college and had white ribbons available for anyone who wanted to wear one. One of the day instructors decided he wanted to have nothing to do with this but instead of saying so, he removed one of the posters from a bulletin board, defaced it, added my name and contact number to the poster, photocopied it and re-hung a few of them on some bulletin boards. Another instructor saw him at the photocopier and asked what he was doing. He said that he wanted no f***ing part of this and we should be drawing attention to violence against men as well. I thought hard about how to respond and in the end, I went to his office with one of the defaced posters and told him someone saw him doing it. He had a sick grin on his face as he was caught in an act of vandalism – well it was what he was doing; only he was taking the coward's way - and started in about violence against men. I told him that if violence against men was an issue he felt strongly about, he should have dealt with it in a more mature manner rather than defacing the poster in such a cowardly manner and then hanging it back, hoping no one would know it was him who did it. That's violence against everyone because it is beyond disrespectful. It's been a month and when he sees me in the hallway, he looks the other way.

1996

Dear diary,

It's the beginning of the new year and we had our annual Christmas dinner for the students. Each year it just seems to get better and the students - by word of mouth from other students – start planning for it at least two months in advance. We also have a few more of the day staff offering to decorate or donate food to the event and some of them join us. It's slow, but attitudes are changing. Yesterday I baked a cake for Marion's birthday but why does baking a cake for a student's birthday deserve a special mention? There's a story but with me there's always a story that is a bit out of the realm of ordinary or straightforward. Since I started teaching in 1992, I meet with every new student within the first week of their studies and we discuss their educational goals. Some students in the day program only come for high school credits but most of my students want to graduate and own a salon someday. Together we establish an educational plan of how we are going to reach that goal. Talking to them about their goals gives me a better understanding of what school means to them and if they decide they are someday going to be salon owners, I can give them special projects that would reflect their interests later in the program. I find they are much more likely to do the required work if later they can work on projects that meet their interests. It takes a lot of work to do that but I found it helps me to know what the student wants.

We set up a progress plan where students keep track of their progress and we meet biweekly to review their progress and set new goals for the next two weeks. Those meetings go very quickly for the ones who are on target and if I need to, I can spend time with the ones who are falling behind or team them up with a student mentor. Diary, you won't believe how well it works because this helps build student accountability and the progress is also used for selecting the student of the month. Every student has a chance each month because I base it on how much progress the student made that month compared to how they did the month before, not how they compare to other students, so even if they didn't make as much progress the previous month, they have a chance the next month. It's amazing how knowing that at the start of every month they have a chance to be selected as the student of the month makes them focus on their studies. I wish when I was growing up we had the same opportunities each month but if you were not a good student at the beginning of the school year, there was little hope for things to turn around because your marks got worse as the term continued. By the end of the school year, your exam was worth 100% of your final grade so you had no chance in hell to succeed unless by some miracle.

I digressed from my Marion story but I had to lay the foundation to the story. During my initial meeting with each student, I also ask about their birthday and record the day and month on my calendar. I decided when I started teaching that every student who comes into my program gets a cake on their birthday. The cakes are not fancy but I think it's important to let every student know their success is important to me. No matter whether the student likes or dislikes me - and I've had a few of those who didn't think I did anything right – they get a cake. So why did I mention Marion's birthday cake? It was guilt which led to decadence. Her birthday was on the same day I was hosting my annual Christmas Dinner for my hairstyling students in my home. I don't think I ever mentioned them but I always have so much to tell you that sometimes I forget what I've said and what I left out. I have to tell you more about that but let me finish my story about Marion. She and I agreed that since the entire class was going to be feasting at my house on her birthday, I would bake her birthday cake on the first day of classes in the new year. And I forgot to bake it! So of course two days ago school started and at dinner time, when no cake emerged from my office, she asked if I had forgotten. I said I did and felt terrible. Imagine your mother or sister forgetting your birthday. She said that was how she felt. So drowning in guilt, I came home and baked the most decadent marbled chocolate and almond cheesecake with a chocolate topping and took it to school yesterday. Everyone was beside themselves with the cake which then led to comparing who got the best ever cake. Marion's cake won out. I told them that guilt speaks volumes but I was not going to forget another birthday cake and I won't.

So let me tell you about the Hairstyling Christmas dinner. This one is just for my students. I started doing it the second year of teaching. I host it at my home and the students are invited but they don't have to cook or bring any food. I do, however, ask them to bring one gift that will cost no money. I give each student a sheet of paper with the names of the entire class and every student is asked to say something good about every other student. My stipulation is that it has to be thoughtful so they can't say someone has nice hair or someone is punctual. I then collect all the filled in sheets and compile the comments for each student and present that as the gift from all the other students. I tell them they can share their comments with the others if they wish to do so and some of them get very emotional and cannot finish their reading. Some of them also said they found it was easy to criticize someone but much harder to find something nice to say but after doing the exercise, they are much more aware of the impact of the hurtful things they say about others. It was a great reminder to some students that they are valued as people.

1997

Dear diary,

Last year was one stressful year that it's hard to know where to start. You know how you hear stories of people in cushy government jobs who don't ever have to work too hard, never have to work overtime and never have to worry about losing their jobs? Well, I sometimes wish that was the case for Robin. He still continues to work hard including overtime and last year with government cutback, he thought he might lose his job. Some of his colleagues took a buy-out offered by the government and left. Robin could not afford to do that because he was only 49 and he would have received a high penalty on his pension because he was not yet 50. There is university tuition for me, Sharm and Sunita so the threat of my losing my job each year and the threat of losing his job last year made for a very stressful year.

1998

Dear Diary,

Do you remember a long time ago when I was telling you about Cheddi and Burnham and all the politics in Guyana in the 1960s? I used to read the signs on the seawall and now that I am taking courses in international education, a lot of things are making sense. The US just released some CIA documents showing that they provided money to the political parties of the PNC and the UF and even the Trade Union Congress during the 1960s so that Cheddi's government could be defeated. The more I learn about American and British foreign policy, the angrier I get that many lives in Guyana were forever changed with what appears to be little or no regard for their value.

A lot of what I am reading about Paulo Freire is making much more sense – like the way I was educated in Guyana and the freedoms we did not get to enjoy because the British and the Americans were meddling in our government. I used to believe in the value of unions but now I don't know what to think. Are they as corrupt as the people they are supposed to be protecting us from? When I was a hairstylist in a non-union environment, I used to think that if only I could work for a company that had a union, I would have better protection, but now that I am a union member, I am not so sure. I thought I was not looking at the big picture so I joined the union's negotiating committee but when I suggested that there should be some input from the general membership, that went over like a lead balloon. When there's negotiating between the union and the employer, it's all so secretive that we are not allowed to share anything in writing. I don't understand why things need to be so adversarial between the two sides. I still have a lot to learn and I don't appear to be learning it fast enough to affect any change.

Dear diary,

I went back to Guyana last September and things have changed a great deal for the better since I was last there in 1985. At that time, Georgetown looked terrible and so did everywhere else. People became so desperate, the crime rates were horrendous and violent crimes were even worse, even till now. I couldn't believe my beautiful country had turned to this. Many Indian families have left and people said that when Cheddi was elected in 1992, things would change, but the country has been plundered for almost 30 years and there is not much infrastructure left. At least basic foodstuff is not still considered contraband some people who left are now returning to Guyana. I think it'll take many years to rebuild the country to its former glory but this is a start.

I went to the Ministry of Education and offered to provide some free assistance for teacher training but they had no interest or desire to do anything. I offered to pay my own expenses to get there but I have not had much luck. Basically I was told that if I want to do anything, I should organize it myself. It's almost 28 years since I left and most of my family is now living in Canada or the US so I don't have many contacts who would be able to help me plan and organize anything for the summer. It would be nice to do some work with the teachers at the Technical Institute because of my vocational background but it's going to be an uphill battle, I think. I was very disappointed but I'll keep trying.

I was invited by the Headmistress of my old school Cumming's Lodge to give a speech at the school's general assembly during the first days of the school year. I don't remember exactly what I said but I do remember saying that those were the most important years of my early life and I formed friendships I still hold close to my heart. I toured the school and was utterly disappointed. The library was gone and the carpentry and drafting programs were minimal at best because thieves had broken into the school and stolen the few pieces of old and rusted tools. The school had twice as many students as when I was attending and the furniture was broken and neglected. The playing field is now grown in and small vendors have set up little businesses in the school yard so that students do not go outside to play because there is no playground but to buy food at recess and lunch. The basic necessities like functioning toilets were absent or working poorly. The water fountain at the back of the school is mossy and dirty. That was truly sad to see. I felt like crying so I had a good cry and then tried contacting my friends through email to ask if they would be willing to donate some money to rebuild a school library. It's hard to know where to start when there is so much to do.

Dear diary,

I'm finished my course work for my master's but I have six major essays to write before I have my oral exam. I decided to do the comprehensive exam route rather than the thesis route because I am not planning to do a PhD at some later date. It's a staggering amount of work to write six more 25-30-page essays for my comprehensive exam after doing ten courses, and with opening a salon at the Riverview Health Centre and working full-time, I hardly have time to think. The salon provides services for long-term care and terminal patients. It's good work but it demands so much of my time that I am feeling like something is going to be sacrificed. I think it's those six papers for now. I always have these grand ideas and big dreams that demand so much time and effort and I have to start thinking things through before jumping in and trying to be and do everything.

1999

Dear diary,

In the last few months, Robin has been having a much better time at work. Months prior to that, he was at the point of going on stress leave because he was being undermined by a staff member who reports to him. Things finally came to a head when the staff member threatened him with physical violence. Robin reported this incident to a regional director who dismissed the threat and threatened to make Robin's life miserable. When Robin finally said that he would hire a lawyer and air the department's dirty laundry, his supervisor reassigned the staff member who made the threats. Things in his department changed considerably for the better when he was assigned an engineer from Egypt to work for him. They are great buddies and find time each day to have a cup of tea together. What was surprising about these bullying and coercive behaviours by his supervisors and staff member was his lack of success when he asked his union to support him. He decided that if things were going to change, he would have to work toward that change so he became a more active union steward.

2000

Dear diary,

A whole year has gone by and a lot has happened. Subhadra started university last September. Sharm has a teaching job in Estevan, Saskatchewan. She completed her Arts degree and a Bachelor of Education degree. She is at a French Immersion Catholic school where she's teaching most subjects in junior high. Sunita is almost done her degree in Environmental Science. She only spent 4 months in Calgary before deciding she was not yet ready to live away from home. Life is moving very quickly and my daughters are growing up into wonderful and very smart young women. I had to close the salon at Riverview last September because it was too much with working full-time, managing the salon and trying to finish my Masters. I finally finished and graduated in February of this year. That's why I have not been writing to you much in the last year. I didn't go to my graduation and I think my family was disappointed but I didn't see the need for a public acknowledgement this time. I rationalized that the Bachelor's degree was an accomplishment for the world and my family. The master's was entirely for my personal satisfaction but along the way, I feel that my students benefitted from my learning.

I got an increase in my salary so I am now one of two of the highest paid teachers at the college, earning the same money as an academic teacher with a PhD. This was made possible because of the combined academic credits for vocational teachers from the teacher certification branch as well as collective agreements which were negotiated to grant credits for years of work. My salary is now significantly more than most vocational teachers who have their vocational teaching certificate from Red River Community College. In some cases it is almost $25,000 more. So my crazy notion in 1991 to pass up a teaching job to go to university was not so crazy after all; it took one year after starting at the university to move to a higher pay scale than I would have earned in 1991 and another two years to move to yet another higher pay scale and then an additional 5 years to move to the highest pay scale that a teacher could achieve because it took me that long to complete my masters. Diary, I am finally seeing the financial rewards of my hard work and studies but I suppose if that was my focus, I may have completed my master's degree 3 years ago. I am also seeing I am becoming bored with teaching. I think I need to do something else but I am not sure what that is. I did several courses in international and cross-cultural education so I think that may be a direction that I could find interesting.

In the last few years, I think I have provided a good learning environment for my students and I know that sometimes I have asked them to do more than the curriculum requires. Every year for the past few years, I have been coaching them for hairstyling competitions and some of them have done very well. Christy is one of the students I am very proud of. She started my program as a mature student who left school in junior high. She worked as a waitress for several years before deciding to go back to school but it was tough for her both financially and academically. I knew that she was going to be a skilled colour technician someday, so she said she wanted to enter a colour competition. I suggested since she was already good at that, she should enter into the perm category by learning to become expert in that area too. I was so proud of her; she won the provincial competition and we raised some funds to send her to Toronto where she won at the national level. She received a scholarship to go to the Vidal Sassoon Academy in New York. What a great success story. I also had a few failures, some of which I dwelled on for a long time, until one of my friends told me to focus on the 95% success rate and stop beating myself up for the 5% that did not succeed. I'm not okay with that but I have also come to realize there are many other mitigating factors influencing student success.

Dear diary,

I have been giving considerably more thought to moving on to something new, perhaps in international education, because I still believe in its educational value especially since we have been a host family for many international students for the last 12 years. With all the travelling I have done to other countries, I've learned how other people live and how lucky I am to be living in Canada even with some of my negative experiences. I think I have done all that I can do in a hairstyling program and it's time to look for new opportunities. Employers are waiting in line for my hairstyling graduates, the students are winning provincial and national hairstyling competitions, the program is generating some revenue for additional supplemental class-room resources, it has a good reputation in the community for volunteer contributions and the program advisory committee is active. So it's time to move on, especially now that I'm sensing something at the college that I am not liking.

I've been hearing some rumblings about closing my program but nothing directly from the administrators. I think it has less to do with the program's popularity and more to do with how much I am getting paid. I can see some of the signs already. Some clients who come to the school to get hair services are saying they are interested in enrolling in the program as a student but when they try to register, they are told registration has been suspended pending further notice. When I ask the director and registrar about enrolments, I am told the numbers are low and there doesn't appear to be any interest. The information I am getting from potential students and the information I am getting from the college don't compute.

I also think my program may be targeted because I am a bit of an activist or at least, I ask difficult questions which administrators don't always want to answer. We had a staff survey back in the Spring and we were asked to be as forthcoming as possible because the feedback would be anonymous. Well, I don't mind signing my name if they ask for feedback but in this case I did not. I wrote that Winnipeg Technical College (the name was changed from South Winnipeg Technical Centre) should realize they have a good niche market for international students wanting to come to Canada to do vocational studies; I also said that we are missing a great opportunity by not teaming up with the Fort Garry School Division who already has a successful international student program and is one of the co-owners of Winnipeg Tech. I wrote about the far-reaching benefits to those involved beyond the obvious financial gains for the college. I wrote that the college should have more visionary leadership to pursue those opportunities. The survey was hardly "anonymous" as it was easy to identify who those particular comments were coming from since I spoke openly about these on other occasions including staff meetings.

Perhaps I should not have been so forthcoming but they asked for honest feedback and now I feel I am being penalized for giving it. Plus I am costing them a lot of money. Haha. So much for open feedback and lifelong learning which the college promotes everywhere. I've come to see that it's easy for administrators to "talk the talk" but when it comes to "walking the talk" it's a different story. Lifelong learning is only good to them if it doesn't cost them more money. My education is benefitting my students directly because if I think of what I knew just after

S Sandra Sukhan

graduating from Red River and what I now know and apply in the classroom, it's such a world of a difference. It's too bad they are so short-sighted that they don't see that even vocational students deserve a good education. At one time I was one of those vocational students so I know how important it is was for me to feel that my teachers and counsellors cared about my learning and well-being.

I have a feeling my time at the college is coming to an end. I am not sure how to feel. My brutal schedule of work, study, business and family commitments have all taken a huge toll on my health for the last few years. I am constantly tired from my periods that are lasting too long and are too heavy; I have no energy because I now have severe anemia and take a power nap in the afternoon before I go to work just so I can get through the day; yet I keep finding every reason not to take some time for myself and attend to my health. It's the guilt of being a woman, I think. I feel like I have to be and do everything for everyone and at the end of the day, I will be nothing to anyone. What is wrong with me? Why would I drive myself so hard and so relentlessly? You know the saying about people being the product of their childhood? Well, in this case, I am the quintessential example of that. Feeling that no matter how hard I worked or how well I did in school, by my parents' standards, I could always do better. I am driven to prove something and I can't tell anymore what that something is.

2001

Dear diary,

We are well into the first few months of the year and I've been forced into making a huge adjustment in my extreme schedule. I guess challenging the status quo comes at a price

156

but you either stand by your principles or you fall by someone else's. The evening hairstyling program closed at the end of December last year. It was no surprise at the end but I wish the administrators had the decency to tell me the real reason my program was shut down rather than the reason they gave – that there was no interest in the program from adult learners. I know that to be untrue because I kept getting calls from potential students – many of them new immigrants and people who work at jobs that don't pay them a living wage. That's the worst part of the layoff. I feel helpless because most of my students are women who are trying to get an education in spite of the challenges they face in their lives every day and I feel an obligation to help because I was one of those women. Hairstyling is quite a gendered, low-status and sometimes low-paying occupation but women choose it anyway. In my case it was because I loved doing hair as I am sure it is for some people but having been in the field for more than 25 years, I see that many women choose it because it's better than the work they are doing and it gives them some hope that with this education, their lives will be better. So why are decisions made about closing a program when there is an obvious need? At the end of the day, the financial books for an educational institution have to be balanced but there has to be some humanity involved in these decisions.

Diary, let me tell you about some of my students so you can understand why I am so upset about the closing of the program. Two of them were sisters who were hairstylists from another country. They wanted to work in Canada as hairstylists but when they went to the apprenticeship office to have their qualifications recognized, they were told it was not possible. The rule is you must complete 1400 hours of in-school instruction in Manitoba before you can write the provincial test. Since they did not complete their schooling in Canada, they were not allowed to write the test. In desperation, they heard from someone that SWTC had a hairstyling teacher (me) who might be willing to help them. After some discussion, we reviewed a competency listing of the practical and theoretical skills for the program and they agreed to identify all the things they believed they were competent at. I randomly tested them on some of the practical skills and they were extremely competent. With the director's approval, they were credited for 1000 hours of the program and came to school for the other 400 hours – mostly theory. They passed the government exam and are now salon owners doing quite well. In a way, we found a way to work around the government regulations that made absolutely no sense. Why should we have been left with only that option when there was a way of giving credit for prior learning? And the biggest irony? The government was promoting recognition of prior learning as a way of equalizing the educational playing field for those who may have apprenticed as a way of learning without benefit of a formal education. That's just one example.

Here are a few more: I worked hard with an immigrant student who did the assessment test and scored at a Grade 2 level but had a great desire to be a hairstylist. I interviewed her and accepted her into the program knowing it would be a lot of extra work for me since there were no student supports at night and English was her second language. I purchased a Spanish textbook for her but in the end she learned from the English one because we agreed she would have to write the government exam in English. She is also now a hairstylist. I had another student who had a young son and wanted to have another baby. She became pregnant and subsequently had a miscarriage at school. I asked another instructor to cover my class so I could take her to the hospital because she had no money for an ambulance. She had just been evicted from her apartment and was living in an unheated trailer in a farmer's field. She left school after that but several years later she contacted me to say she was diagnosed with terminal cancer and wanted to let me know she appreciated everything I had done for her. Another student left an abusive relationship and one night I hid her in my office so that when her boyfriend who was stalking her came to see her, I boldly lied and told him she had already left school; her family came a short time later to take her home. I had another student who was into self-mutilation. I thought she must have had a very vicious cat until her counsellor told me she was doing this to herself. Up till then, I had never heard of such a thing. I went home and read about it on the internet. Some of my students' experiences are so foreign to me. Sometimes I feel I have lived a very sheltered and privileged life. And I have. In many ways, I grew up with privileges I did not need to acknowledge because I never had to think about it. But now that I am teaching, a whole new world has opened up to me – some of it not so good. You see, diary, I made a lot of accommodations for my students because, as with adult learners, many of them were dealing with issues unrelated to the hairstyling content and I wonder if the administrators thought of any of that when they decided to close the program. It's the seeming lack of compassion and humanity in the decisions that dumbfound me. Would it have made any difference if someone in authority knew any of this?

At the end of the day, I am sure it came down to the amount of money I was being paid versus giving someone an opportunity for a better life. And sad to say, my union once again, did nothing to support me. It was even worse this time because I had seniority over another instructor whose position I could have taken but my union did nothing. And there are some lines I will not cross. A few teachers told me to demand the union represent me fairly by asking I be given the other position ahead of the other instructor, but I would not do that because the other instructor was a very close colleague and I would feel I was betraying our friendship. I was also fortunate that Robin was earning a good salary and while I would lose a full-time salary, we had no mortgage and we had enough money to pay for Sunita and Subhadra's university tuition. Financially we were doing fine through careful money management but emotionally, I was hurt that after years of dedication to my teaching, it appears that I was simply a cost the school could not afford.

In retrospect, being laid off was a blessing in disguise although at the time it did not feel like that. The layoff forced me to re-evaluate my priorities and I can now take some time to relax and catch up on some of the things I neglected over time – my health being on the top of that list. The crazy schedule I was living the last few years finally caught up with me. Health-wise, I am feeling great, because I finally had the necessary surgery that probably saved my life. A hysterectomy is not fun but the doctor telling me that I had some precancerous cells in my cervix made me go ahead with the surgery I had been putting off for years. It's been ten years of dealing with anaemia and feeling tired all the time. I attributed it to my hectic schedule but I neglected my health terribly because I thought I needed to be there for my family and my students. Work/life balance is not something I do well. I plunge head-first into work and the life balance is about taking care of everyone ahead of me. I promised it would change so a few days after my surgery I started walking a few feet each day and now I have signed up to walk a half marathon at the Manitoba marathon in June. I can't do things in small measure. Sometimes it's a blessing; other times a torment.

I spent the last two months looking for a teaching position but to no avail. I've gone for two interviews but both principals said I should go back to school and get some additional credentials. I know it has more to do with how much it would cost to hire me. A hairstyling teacher with a Master's degree is surely an anomaly because I am at the top of the pay scale for all teachers in the province and even if I teach English or some other subject, the school division could hire a teacher right out of university and pay them almost $25,000 less than they would have to pay me. And here it was that I wanted to go to school to learn without considering the big picture that eventually I would price myself right out of a teaching job. Another life lesson about what's fair, what's right, what's practical and what's not.

2002

Dear diary,

At the end of the school year in June last year, I finally got a job with the Transcona-Springfield School Division. They hired me half-time to set up a new international education program but I have a very small budget to work with so I have to be very creative in putting an infrastructure in place, from a marketing plan to promotional materials and all the necessary forms. I have been travelling a lot in the last few months. After harping at Winnipeg Tech about the value of international education and how nearsighted it was not to start a program there, I am finally doing it in another school division. It's been a lot of work setting it up and since it's only half-time, I am spending a lot of my own time working at it. In essence, it's a full-time job with a half-time salary but it's exciting. I went to Taiwan to do some promotions based on my friend Holly's references and I also went to Mexico. I can see how I'm a small fish in the huge ocean of international education because my promotional materials are not as sophisticated as others I've seen.

Some school representatives in Winnipeg are going to several educational fairs in other countries that cost thousands of dollars. I am quickly realizing my idealized vision of international education is considerably different from what I am seeing. The fairs look more like cut-throat business endeavours that have little to do with education and more to do with how much profit it makes for school divisions. Some school divisions in Winnipeg are boasting of profits in the hundreds of thousands of dollars and I know from being a host family for Holly so many years ago that some international students pay in excess of $30,000 per year to get an education in Canada. I now have to think like a business person rather than an educator and more and more I am realizing the two can't operate in harmony.

With the recent announcement by the provincial government that the Transcona-Springfield School Division will be split into two, with the Transcona part amalgamating with River East School Division, I can already see the writing on the wall. The amalgamation was very contentious and River East School Division is not pleased with inheriting the Transcona portion of the school division because Transcona is considered a working-class neighbourhood with many railway workers living in that community. The consultant in charge of international education in that school division is very competitive and I don't see her wanting to share her responsibilities with me.

Dear diary,

It is the end of another year and I now have two married daughters. Sharm and Trent got married in the summer and Sunita and Mike were married a few days ago. My family is getting more cosmopolitan each day. Trent is Mennonite and his family has lived in Manitoba for more than one hundred years. I'm learning a great deal about Mennonites. They have a long history of pacifism and they ended up in Manitoba and many places in the world because they were persecuted for their religious beliefs. Mike is Filipino and his parents came to Canada during a time when Canada needed nurses. Mike was born in Edmonton and has lived there all his life. If I had to guess a few years ago that my daughters would marry a Mennonite and a Filipino instead of a Guyanese Indian, I'd have guessed wrong. My two sons-in-law are two of the best men I have met in a long time. I would be proud to say I raised them but I cannot take the credit for them being good people. They are wonderful to my daughters and respectful to us and it's the best thing I could hope for in in-laws.

2003

Dear diary,

The world of international education is so foreign to me. I took several graduate courses in university – none of which prepared me for this extremely competitive world. It's as if all international students have dollar signs attached to them. I feel like the poor orphaned cousin in this "family" of schools. You should see some of the promotional literature for some school divisions! They must have spent tens of thousands of dollars. I am getting a lesson in market shares and head counts. I am wholly disappointed because I thought students would come to Canada and there would be this sharing of culture and experiences but that is hardly the case. Most of the students I am marketing to in other countries are high school students and some parents are willing to pay whatever the costs to have their children come to Canada. I am finding out some harsh realities. Some parents are so wealthy and they have little or no interest in managing their children so international education is seen as a cheaper version of an exclusive boarding school experience.

One of the most troubling observations for me is the privilege some people enjoy because of the money they have. The topic of privilege has been particularly fascinating for me ever since I took a course with Laara Fitznor in 1995 on cross-cultural and anti-racist education but the evidence is so glaring that it is hard to overlook or discount anymore. I am marketing international education to very wealthy families and most of the time I think of it as a job somehow separate from my life but the more I see how money can buy anything, the more I dislike my work. Laara herself is Aboriginal and I think most of us identified with her – at least I did – and some of the experiences she had. I recall when she first introduced us to Peggy McIntosh's article on *White Privilege: Unpacking the Invisible Knapsack*. There were only a few white students in the course and there were no men but the discussions were heated and lasted almost the entire course. Some students felt defensive and some felt victimized and several times we were talking past each other instead of listening. It was startling to see such extreme points of view but it was also the first time in 1995 that I really could think of my experiences growing up in Guyana and how the British government divided and conquered our country by pitting Blacks against Indians.

At the time Laara was teaching, I could totally relate to the privileges I didn't have as a new immigrant to Canada but now I am rethinking my perspective on privilege. I know I felt vindicated that my experiences when I first came to Canada were real, especially when I think back of the way Mr. Henderson treated me. I now recognize that what I was experiencing was prejudice, discrimination and culture shock – only at the time I did not have a name for it, nor would I have known how to deal with it. In Laara's course, I felt the righteous indignation at my own victimization as an immigrant in Canada but in the last ten years, I've had a lot to think about. I see that international education is only for the wealthy. I say that because I had the most heartfelt experience when I was travelling. I was staying at a hotel where the educational fair was being held and I stopped at the front desk to talk to one of the staff members. His English was exceptionally good so I asked where he learned English. He said it was mostly from watching television because he could not afford to go to an English school. I casually told him he could go to Canada and study and he asked about the tuition and accommodation costs. When I told him that it was in excess of $20,000 Canadian per year, he looked shocked and said that in two years, he'd never be able to make that money – and he considered that he was paid very well for the position he was in, because of his ability to speak English. I went back to my room that night disquieted by my conversation earlier. It was just such a thoughtless thing for me to say.

The whole question of privilege is filled with contradictions. On further exploration of other kinds of privileges through articles by Robert Jensen, bell hooks, and other authors, I have to face the fact that I am also implicated in the silence around my own privilege of class and race when I was growing up in Guyana. Growing up in a privileged life in Guyana, I really had no awareness I was privileged. I simply assumed everyone lived the way I did and I didn't question that I had more than many others. If my friends were wanting and I had, I would simply share whatever I could, and of course I expected they would do the same for me if ever I needed it. That was the part I didn't question – that I never seemed to need anything from them, at least nothing material. The idea of privilege was connected to class and race as well but I didn't see that either. Now it's not so easy to be judgmental of others without looking at myself too. And so, casually telling the desk person he could go to Canada to study was very insensitive. Diary, I strive to be a good person but there are times when I want to box myself at the side of the head for saying the stupidest things.

Diary, I am thinking back to two years ago when I went to Toronto for Beatrice's daughter's wedding. I met Racey there. I don't think I ever talked about Racey or Beatrice and Chead. These are my friends who I went to Cumming's Lodge school with since 1965 and after more than 30 years, we are still friends. Anyway, I met Racey and his wife at the wedding and he was telling his wife a story about when we first started in Form 1 at Cumming's Lodge in 1965. Apparently sometime during the first week of school, I asked him why he came to school barefoot every day and he said his parents had no money to buy shoes. The next day I arrived at school with my brother's slippers and told him he could have them. He also reminded me of the time in Second Form we had a school dance and he didn't have the 10 cents to pay to attend so three of us gave him the money so he could attend. He asked if I remembered any of it and I did not. I laughed when he was telling the story but it made me think of how I took my good life for granted. I suppose back then, 10 cents was nothing to me but he said that to him it was the best thing that had ever happened and he never forgot it, even more than 30 years later.

Sometimes I think back to those days and realize how very important they were to me. I still keep in touch with many of those friends and we try to have a reunion whenever we can, but most of us are so scattered around the world that it's hard to meet in person. I use email a lot now and I hope I'll soon be able to create an alumni website so we can continue to raise money for books and supplies for Cumming's Lodge. It's funny that I attended Massey and spent years as a parent volunteer in all my children's schools including Massey, but I don't attend the reunions or other alumni events. However, I do my utmost to attend anything for Cumming's Lodge or to keep in touch with my friends from there.

Dear diary,

First the good news; I have a new baby granddaughter, Izabel Anjali. Sunita asked my opinion about an Indian name and we both came up with Anjali. She has the most beautiful head of hair I have even seen. I thought no one in the world could have children as beautiful as mine but I can see my granddaughter is equally as beautiful. I cannot believe I am now a grandmother. When she is able to talk, I'll ask her to call me Nani which is your mother's mother in Hindi. I guess every ethnic group has their favourite name for grandmother and grandfather but I don't know why I didn't insist that my children call my parents

Nani and Nana. I had a Nani and Nana but my kids said Grandpa and Grandma.

Another interesting piece of news: Winnipeg Technical College has re-opened the evening Hairstyling program. How convenient that they waited long enough for me not to be able to grieve the re-opening and ask for my position and they can now pay a new teacher at a much lower salary. All the talk about how the enrollment numbers were not there was only that – talk. I have moved on to better things but I can't help but think about the way I was pushed out after what I believed was dedication and commitment to my work. I can say though that when I see students who have graduated (and some who did not), they have good things to say about their time in my program so I let that be my solace. Had I not been pushed out, I may not have realized there was a whole world or other interesting experiences waiting for me to discover.

2004

Dear diary,

It's been a long time since I shared my world with you and a lot has happened. As I expected, the Transcona-Springfield School Division was split and the Transcona part amalgamated with River East to become the River East-Transcona School Division. I moved there but the next year, in an effort to get rid of my position, the board asked me if I wanted to be a home-stay co-ordinator instead of a director at half the salary I was getting paid in the previous position. It was such an affront that I went to speak to the Superintendent. He made all the clichéd platitudes about how my contributions to the division were important and how much my efforts were appreciated. I don't even think he knew my name prior to my asking for an appointment with him. I had seen him in the hallway but he only ever nodded his head in my direction. I asked if the school division would reconsider the decision to offer me the "slap-in-the-face" home-stay coordinator's position but he said the decision was made. I declined the offer and decided to leave the division.

Diary, I have to tell you that the world works in mysterious ways. As if by serendipity, at almost the same time I decided to leave the school division, I received a call from Pam asking me if I would be interested in a half-time term position in her depart-ment. She is now the manager of the Program and Curriculum Development department at Red River Community College. My life has come full circle – again. She offered me a term posi-tion in her department to work on a program renewal with one of the consultants and she is now my supervisor. It was great because I could work from home and only needed to go in to the college for meetings. While I was working on the project, I happened to see Jim McKay who is the chair of the Teacher Education program and we started to talk about the lack of access to education for many people. He said he had been fol-lowing my career path since I graduated from his program and offered me a wonderful opportunity to teach in the Certificate of Adult Education program – the same one from which I had graduated. When I completed my Vocational Teaching Certificate at Red River, I also received a concurrent Certificate of Adult Education. He suggested I might be interested in pilot-ing some of the CAE courses by streaming video and if I was, I should go to the TV studio and speak to the manager.

I went to talk to Dave in the TV studio and he explained how streaming video worked. Basically I would be in a TV studio with some students and the others would log on to their computers and see the video on the internet. I have never done anything like this. The closest I ever came was me putting a video camera in my classroom to record how I interact with students throughout the day. I was the only one reviewing it so there was no anxiety about looking silly. That experience made me a better teacher because it showed me how frequently and why I was interacting with some students and not so much with others. Well diary, I started teaching by streaming video and Dave said I took to the camera so naturally that he was sure I had done this before. We work really well as a team; I come up with my "pie in the sky" ideas about pedagogy and he is a technical wizard so we are making it happen. Dave was a genius as he worked out the challenging technical details like bandwidth which are beyond me, but we are now streaming to some of the regional campuses as well as to Assiniboine Community College and University College of the North. That's pretty exciting that students can access courses without having to leave their communities. For many people in northern and rural communities, this is a gift and little by little, we are breaking down those barriers they face.

Dear diary,

Late last Spring, just after I decided to leave international education, I received a call from another school division wanting to hire me to start up an international education program in their division on a half-time basis. We had a lengthy discussion about my philosophy about international education and I made it clear I was not interested in simply generating profits for the division without putting the appropriate infrastructure in place as well as the cultural sensitivity training for the front end staff the international students would be interacting with. I was told that since I was the one with the experience, I could set up the program any way I wanted. After I agreed, I was told that since there was not a lot of money for the international education program, I would be hired as a .3 position for the Aboriginal Achievement program and .2 for the international program. That amounted to one day a week for the international program which was not sufficient realistically.

I was supposed to start at the beginning of the school year in September but I ended up starting work full-time in early July without pay and by the time September arrived, I had already done a lot without compensation. How do I get myself into these situations? I attended recruitment fairs in three cities in Brazil and three in Mexico in the Fall and I met with agents and potential host families. I spent no time on the Aboriginal program. I believe that there was really no intention for me to do any work for that program even though the school division included an aboriginal reserve with a large number of aboriginal students in the division's programs. Government funding was provided specifically for that purpose but it was spent in my salary in international education which was not funded because it was a "for-profit" program.

Diary, you'd think I would learn how to play those political games but I don't learn some things well so instead of playing the game, I got frustrated that much of the infrastructure I was trying to put in place was being subverted by other staff members and my vision for the program was once again going off in a different direction from my intended purpose. So, I resigned on the last teaching day in December. I have now completely wrecked my back from lifting heaving suitcases for many months while marketing the program overseas. I am so incapacitated, barely able to walk let alone travel anywhere and I feel myself getting more and more isolated from family and friends. One bright note these last few months was the birth of my second grandbaby, Sahana to Sharm and Trent. She has the cutest little heart-shaped face.

.4.

⁓

2005

Dear diary,

This Spring while I was teaching part-time and trying to recuperate from my back injuries, I had a lot of time to think about my future and what I wanted it to look like. Since I've been teaching at Red River College, (the name was changed a few years ago but I still sometimes refer to it as a community college), I am really beginning to see how much work still needs to be done if vocational students are to get the best education they deserve. I think the teacher education program is good, but has some limitations and I don't think that's just at Red River; my experiences at the U of M made me realize they are not preparing vocational teachers sufficiently for classroom experiences. I am also troubled by the way we as teacher-educators fail to prepare our teachers and that includes me as one of those teacher-educators.

I feel like I don't know enough about what I don't know – kind of like the cultural awareness exercise that I do with my students where there are four levels of awareness. Level 1 is you are not aware that you are not aware; Level 2 – You are aware that you are not aware; Level 3 – you are aware that you are aware; and Level 4 – you are unaware that you are aware. I think for the most part, I am functioning at Level 3 but there are times I know I am at Level 2 and of course, if I am at a Level 1, I wouldn't even know that. The courses I teach in Diversity and Inclusiveness and on the Foundations of Education are the most challenging especially when I raise some issues which teachers either don't want to or can't be bothered to address. When I raise topics that are uncomfortable, some of them think it isn't their responsibility to deal with them. The Diversity course is particularly difficult because some of the teachers don't seem to care, or they think it's my cause or issue because I am a woman of colour. Some teachers have made personal verbal attacks to me in the classroom and through assignments and some of them believe when I am teaching by streaming video, they can write anything in the chat feature because they are not face-to-face with me. In one case it was so utterly disrespectful I had to start communicating through my course outline that some of the topics being presented in the course may be controversial but the discussion should always be done respectfully - and that includes respect for the instructor. I think of how far I have come with issues of race relations but I also see how much farther we as a society still have to go.

I found an interesting book that I took on vacation last year and thought it might be a good book to use in the Diversity course. The title is *Seeing Ourselves,* written by Carl James, who is a professor at York University. It is not an easy text to read and if you are a white male who may not yet be at a stage where you can acknowledge the systemic privileges many white people enjoy, then it is an even harder text to read because the stories are about the experiences of student teachers, some of which may not be good experiences. In one particular class, a student was so offended by what he was reading, he accused the author of being racist and said the author should be fired for his views on racism. I pointed out that the author had grounded his work on research of the historical and current policies that Canada had used to keep out people who did not look Caucasian or more specifically, British or French. The student disagreed with me so I suggested he contact the university with his evidence of the author's racism and make a case for firing him. The student declined but I decided to contact the author myself and invite him via telephone as a guest speaker in the course.

We had a great discussion and I told him I had applied to York's Faculty of Education a few months prior to do a PhD but my application had been rejected. He said that given my background in adult and vocational education and my experiences as a tradesperson, I should apply to the Master's program at the Faculty of Environmental Studies at York, because I could design my own program of studies and when I start, I can apply to the PhD program for the next year. I decided it was time to go back to school so I took his advice and applied. To my great surprise, I was accepted into the Master's program. I'll start in September and Laara Fitznor, my professor at the U of M, told me that when I go there, I should contact Celia Haig-Brown because she'd be a good person to get to know in the Faculty of Education. My life has taken another turn as if by accident, but I think its serendipity. I've come to believe that things happen in my life for a reason and I am where I am supposed to be because it's the right time. The logistics of this is yet to be worked out because although Robin has been supportive so far, I think going to Toronto to study was not part of the arrangement and might take a bit more negotiating. I've always managed to do my studies while juggling competing priorities, but this time, I may have the chance for the first time in my post-secondary education to be a full-time student.

Dear diary,

I am now enrolled in the Masters of Environmental Studies at York University. It's been quite an adjustment leaving my home in Winnipeg to come here to study and it's going to be expensive to maintain two homes, but I got a Graduate Assistantship which was a pleasant surprise when I got my acceptance letter. It's not much but it will help pay for some of my expenses for my studies. I am lucky to have family and some of my long-time friends from Cumming's Lodge living in Toronto so I'll be able to spend some time with them while I'm there.

It just occurred to me that except for Hairstyling School in the 70s, none of my post-secondary education has been as a full-time student. It is a great experience so far and I am thrilled to be here. For the first time since I left Guyana at 16, I can focus on school without the other life obligations. Did I say I was excited? Yes I am! Only thing is, I left my comfortable house in Winnipeg to come to Toronto and I am now officially a full-time student living in student housing on campus – a first for me – but it's a cute loft apartment for graduate students with a little front yard. I only have to think about me and my studies. My kids are all grown up and have their own lives. Sharm and Sunita have been married for three years; Subhadra moved to her own place last year so I feel that my work as a parent has moved to another life stage. We divided the assets from the two revenue homes between the three girls and gave them each one third of the proceeds. Sharm and Trent bought one of the houses, Subhadra the other and Sunita and Mike used their portion to buy a home in Edmonton. I am very glad that they all finished university with no student debts so they are free to start earning a living without student loans hanging over them. Finally I can focus all of my attention on being a student and I will have lots of time to study instead of squeezing out every bit of time each day. Over the years I have become so extremely efficient at managing my time that my friend Brent often jokes I must have a clone of me because one person could not get done in a day what I seem to be able to do. I laugh when he says that but sometimes I take on too much and drive myself hard to meet my commitments.

My course work is exceptionally heavy and we are expected to read about 500 pages each week. I can barely keep up and all my ambitions of visiting friends and family have gone out the window. Between my readings and calling home or to the kids, I am managing but extra time is not available. I seem to be the only one doing ALL of the course readings but diary, you most of all know how I can become obsessive about doing what is expected. Would anyone know or care if I didn't do a course reading? Probably not. It's not so much that I would care that my professors would be disappointed; it's more that I feel if I don't do it, I may miss out on learning something really important. I was a voracious reader before but now I have become positively over-zealous.

Dear diary,

I am taking this course called Development Studies and although it is interesting, I have to work really hard to follow some of the themes. Many of the students have a background of undergraduate courses in this area so I am feeling at a distinct disadvantage. I don't think the teacher is interested in what I have to say because he seems to dismiss what I am saying with a nod of the head and then he is on to his next preferred student. Anyway, the course assignment is making me read some texts that I would not have read before so that's good. I wrote a paper on the effects of colonialism on developing countries, especially its long-lasting effects on Guyanese still living in Guyana. I also wrote about the hegemony of the World Bank and the

International Monetary Fund and the impact of the imposition of structural adjustment programs which have now created new generations of underclass Guyanese with a mentality of dependence. I remember as a child how proud we were to be self-sufficient and now Guyana is a place of despair with sky-rocketing crime and drugs. The Americans have now released secret CIA documents which clearly state that during the 1960s, they helped Burnham to get and stay in power. American foreign policies have changed the lives of so many people and in many cases, not for the better but somehow they are not held accountable.

I think back to reading about how Paulo Freire was fighting for the rights of the poor in Brazil at the same time that Dr. Jagan was fighting for Guyana's right to self-government. I was proud because Dr. Jagan was a family friend and our dentist and later became the President in Guyana, and in over 30 years of near political exclusion, he never gave up fighting for his beliefs. I read his address to the United Nations General Assembly in 1995 offering his solution for a New Global Human Order and it sounded so similar to those I heard as a child. Diary, I think back to how I used to hide behind the door and listen to Dad talking about how Uncle Boysee was imprisoned; it was only a few years ago when I went back to visit Guyana and was talking to Cousin Ralph that I came to know he was imprisoned without a trial because of his efforts to fight for the freedom, liberation and democratic rights of many poor and marginalized people. That was the same year I was born and after years of whispers, I can finally know that Uncle Boysee and many like him laid the foundation for my life and for many others like me by standing by their beliefs even when it meant having their freedom stolen from them.

I am confident that those experiences of my childhood influenced me at some level. Having listened to political speeches as a child, the messages resonated in me for years and I believe it was part of the reason I feel compelled to give back in whatever way I can and to be passionate about fighting for the rights of those who cannot fight for themselves. Many of these life lessons make me critically aware that I need to self-interrogate. Sometimes I think I should be doing more, but when I ask myself the question, "Why do/don't I get involved?" I think there is a certain amount of discomfort in the answers. Asking and answering the question means I have to do more than care. I have to get involved. And I once heard you have to pick your battles but when there are so many, it's hard to prioritize them and I don't want to choose the easiest road just because it may offer a quick solution. Some things are worth fighting for and some of those fights may never end.

Diary, I have to tell you about Chris. He, undoubtedly, has to be one of my greatest teachers. He is so smart about so many things that I feel that even with all my life's experiences, his life is so rich and interesting. He is teaching a course in Popular Education. Prior to starting this program, I had never even heard the phrase but I have now come to know that much of what I was doing with and for my students in the last 15 years would be considered popular education. I often use story-telling as a way of learning and I recall a couple of years ago while teaching in the CAE program that some of the student feedback on my course was very negative because they felt I should stop telling so many stories and get on with the business of teaching about lesson plans. At first I was a bit disturbed by the comments but Chris has given me the vocabulary for much of what bell hooks refers to as *eros* – not being afraid to love your students; she advocates for being a caring teacher who is at ease with nurturing her students. Chris taught me that story-telling is part of the oral traditions of many cultures handed down from generation to generation by elders to the young of their communities. I feel like I've just discovered some of my long-lost family with some of the students and teachers I've just met.

Dear diary,

My first semester is over and I am spending the next month at home. I am glad to be at school but this is the first time I have ever, ever lived on my own. It's a bit lonely so I am glad to be in my comfy bed and the best part of being home is not having to walk across the courtyard to do my laundry. Christmas is going to be great. It'll be busy but I'm looking forward to the holidays and to Christmas lunch this year. It'll be a much smaller crowd this year – about 10 or 12 of us. Diary, do you remember about 10 years ago when I had about 30 people for Christmas lunch and we had to get two extra eight- foot tables and set them up in the living room? Times have changed. My kids have kids of their own but we still like to gather at home here for the special occasions.

2006

Dear diary,

It's now the end of February and I am in in a state of total disbelief. I went back to Winnipeg all excited to celebrate Dad's 75th birthday as well as my birthday and I got the greatest shock of my life. Dad told us after his birthday pooja that he has cancer in his right eye – to be more specific – cancer of the lacrimal sac. What the hell is a lacrimal sac? Dad wasn't clear either but what he did know was what the doctors told him –that the cancer was bad and they would have to remove his eye. I went home and did some research and found out that the lacrimal sac was the tear duct in his eyes. Who gets cancer in a tear duct, for God's sake? I also found out that it's an extremely rare form of cancer – so rare that one in approximately 300,000 people get it. There is very little data and research on this kind of cancer so the doctors have no idea how it might behave. They said that cancer has already advanced to stage 4 which is the worst stage and it has invaded his nasal bones. They told him to act quickly to have the surgery but I am trying to look for some alternative treatments that may save his eye. The problem as the doctors explained it is that his eye is perfectly fine but there will be no eye socket left to support the eye or even a prosthetic eye.

I feel numb, as if I am walking in a bad dream and someone will wake me up and tell me that it was only a dream. I went back to York hardly able to concentrate on what to do next. I always have a back-up plan and a back-up to the back-up plan, but this time, I have no idea what I should be doing. What if we wait for an alternative treatment and it's too late? What if we do the surgery and then find out after Dad has lost his eye that it may not have been necessary? Whatever the decision, one of them is not to do nothing and hope that it'll go away. I think for the next few days, I walked in a fog, hardly able to think about a next step. How do you plan for a next step when someone tells you that you have cancer and you are about to lose your eye? Diary, You must be thinking I am not making much sense because I am making it sound like I am the one with the cancer but it feels like that. So much of my life has been wrapped up in Dad's life – I mean from the very day I was born – that sometimes it's hard to separate what's his life and what's mine.

I spoke to the Graduate Program director and asked if I could finish my semester early and I'll go back to Winnipeg. I am not sure if I will be able to continue my studies so for now, I am expecting to finish the three courses I am taking at York and I'll see where I go from here. I withdrew from the U of Toronto course because I cannot afford the time to go there once a week and still finish these courses. Somehow my studies don't seem so important in the whole scheme of things. You can plan your life as carefully as you want but when something like this comes along, you reconsider your priorities. I am usually so sure of my decisions when I make them, but this time, my father's life depends on it – quite literally; he trusts me so implicitly to make the right decision that I have now become immobilized by my inability to make a decision for or against the surgery.

Dear diary,

I finished my semester early by being focused enough to complete all my coursework. February and March were the hardest two months I have experienced in a long time. While I was doing that, I was communicating with a few doctors, one particular doctor in Vancouver who said he would be able to save Dad's eye. I came back to Winnipeg at the end of March and just a day before Dad left for a consultation with the doctor, he was told that the doctor reviewed the file and the cancer had progressed way beyond the stage where he could help, so the decision was made for the eye to be removed. Disappointment was evident for all of us because we already had a plan in place for the minor surgery and recuperation time in Vancouver. That was all thrown out the window and we lost two precious months.

In the end, after much research and a few hopeful possibilities, we were left with only one choice – that Dad needed to have the surgery. He was really brave when we were discussing options. By the middle of April, we met with the oncologist to decide on a date for the surgery. The doctor said he and his team would remove Dad's eye and excavate his nose. What a term! Excavate! I don't even know if that was the right word they used but that's what I heard. They said that they would cut a part of his leg and graft it to the eye area so that eventually there would not be a sunken hollow where his eye should be. The whole conversation was surreal and I can barely imagine what Dad must have been thinking. You have no idea how dispirited I was. This is a man who has always been careful about his appearance and that of his family and that we had to look good at all times – all of us. At all times and most especially in public. These were our standards in our growing up years and it continues to be his and mine. It sounds superficial but Dad said when he was a young-ster and his mom passed away when he was only 14, his uncle used to tell him that it doesn't matter how poor he is, he should always, always strive to be well-groomed and I don't remember him being otherwise.

Dear diary,

I am learning to negotiate the health care system. I have become preoccupied with searching for information about cancer and how to manage it. The internet has become my best friend, well, that is, except for you. My research skills are paying off because I am a fiend when it comes to finding information. I am also glad I am super- organized because I do not go to a doc-tor's appointment without Dad's journal that I make him take to every appointment with any health care practitioner. I find this helps me to capture what the health care practitioners are saying so that later I can make sense of the conversations and I can search for some of the words that are new to me. I am learning a whole new vocabulary and I am learning more than anything else that when someone is going through something this serious, it is best to have an advocate who can accompany them to appointments and meetings.

After all the hard work and desperate search to find another alternative, Dad had his surgery at the beginning of June and he is doing better than anyone expected. The surgery was more than 9 hours and he lost his right eye and part of his nose. He was remarkably courageous before and after the surgery. I stayed at the hospital most of the day except for a brief period when I took Mom home after we bid him goodbye at the surgery doors. I could not stay away and imagined that if I wasn't there, something would go wrong. Thank goodness nothing did, but his face looked horribly disfigured from the handsome face we all knew. He rationalized that if the cost of living was an eye, he was willing to pay the price. He used to tell us when we were little that in the world of the blind man, the one-eyed man was king. I reminded him of that and jokingly asked if this wasn't a bit extreme on his part to seek a coronation. That was my attempt at humour and fortunately he was able to laugh about it.

So what about my schooling all this time? Well, it took somewhat of a backseat in my life because there was so much to deal with, but Dad recovered so well and so fast that it gave me the opportunity to continue my summer semester. In the Spring, I searched many databases for an internship which was a requirement for my program of studies but most places don't offer them to anyone over 30. Maybe when you get to my age, they don't think you have much time left or that you can't contribute to society in a meaningful way. It's the ageism bias of this culture to privilege youth over maturity and experience. I finally got one with World University Services of Canada's Students Without Borders to do an internship in Botswana and decided I would only go if Dad recovered from his surgery enough for me not to worry about him.

I accepted the internship and left for Botswana in early July. Before the application, I knew that Botswana was somewhere in Africa but I don't think I could have picked it out on a map. I spent two months there and it was a great learning experience for me. I went with some stereotypical and preconceived ideas of what I would contribute and what I would leave behind; I intended to do my major paper for my Master's degree on preparing students for international/intercultural internships, but I think because of my experiences at the training centre in Gaborone, I intend to do my final paper on sustainability education in the context of technical and vocational education. I think I'll ask Chris Cavanagh to be my supervisor for my final paper. He really is totally awesome and was very compassionate and understanding while Dad was ill.

Dear diary,

I am now back in Toronto and Dad is doing very well. He recovered from the surgery better than the doctors expected but he had to get 30 rounds of radiation. The doctors said they got all of the cancer but they did the radiation just to make sure that if there is even one cell left, it will be killed. Mom and Dad are now with me in my little apartment on campus. He is a bit weak from the radiation so they'll spend a couple weeks with me recuperating and just spending time together. It has eased my mind greatly to have him here because I can tend to him and make sure he eats and get sufficient rest.

I have started my fourth semester and I plan to complete my studies in five semesters rather than six. Diary, I had an experience while I was Botswana that I cannot get out of my head. Remember I told you I went there for the internship? Well I was supposed to help the training centre with a marketing plan to promote training opportunities for under-, and unemployed youths. Those youths weren't just unemployed; they were the poorest of the poor and most of them lived in Old Naledi which is a slum at almost the outskirts of Gaborone. I dislike the word "slum" because of the connotation that the residents are the marginalized and excluded underclass of society.

Diary, the students were so wonderful and taught me so much but I think the most precious gift I got from them was when they named me Mama Sandra. I heard them referring to the centre's director by one name, the teachers by another name and me by Mama. When I asked what the difference was, they explained they use a formal greeting for the director who was an authority figure; they use familial greetings of auntie for the teachers and they call me Mama because they think of me as the mother they don't have. You see, diary, many of them do not have mothers because they died from HIV/AIDS and the young men and women are left as orphans to be raised by grandparents – if there are any around who care about them or who are not already taking care of other grandchildren. Tshepo explained that because of the way I started helping and teaching them in the kitchen and in the computer room, she and the other students felt that if they had a mother who was still alive, she would be like me. That has to be the highest honour that I can be given – to be thought of as their mother, not a mother figure but their mother. I had not had such an experience before except with my own children. As part of my application to WUSC, I have to blog about the experience so I have been writing on the Students Without Borders blog almost every day. If you were a person, I'd tell you to read about it, diary, but I tell you much more than I write on the blog. I tell you all of my emotions – sadness, joy, confusion, anger – all of it and you have the ability to be cathartic for me.

Dear diary,

I wanted to tell you about this conversation I had with a student at the training centre while I was in Gaborone, but I needed to figure out how I was going to explain it to you so that's why I took so long to tell you. I could hardly make sense of it but slowly I am figuring it out. I think this may take the rest of my life because just when I think I understand something clearly, there is another life lesson for me to learn. The conversation seemed rather ordinary at the moment but became increasingly perplexing the longer I thought about it. I had been working with the staff and the students on a marketing plan for the centre. Through a contact at the University of Botswana who suggested I contact one of the local radio stations about getting some free air time, I managed to get an interview. The interview lasted about 30 minutes and was uneventful but it was very valuable and certainly welcome since we had no money to pay for publicity.

I went back to the training centre after the interview and the students were sitting around a little transistor radio where they listened to the interview earlier. They started cheering Mama Sandra for doing such a good job of promoting the centre and they said they felt proud. One of the students came over and hugged me and said she was really proud to call me Mother and her next sentence was the one that threw me off. Her exact words were, "Mama Sandra, we are so proud of you. We know you got the interview because you are White because if you were Black, the radio station would not be interested to talk to you." I immediately repudiated her statement that I was White but of all the things I could claim about me as a person, being White was not one of them.

I think I was uncomfortable with the label of White because in my estimation, to be White is to have some special privilege that others do not have. You see, diary, I have been teaching a course in Diversity and Inclusiveness and one of the topics I cover in that course is White Privilege – that is, the unearned privileges one gets simply from the colour of one's skin. Since taking the Cross-Cultural Education course in my graduate studies, more than ten years ago, I've had a lot of time to think about what White Privilege looks like from the perspective of the one who is without that privilege. I grew up with White people in Guyana and I witnessed the privileges they enjoyed and how we as Indians were considered "less than" White people. I thought back to Mr. Jury and how he used to sit in his car and wait for a child to come along to open the gate to his yard and how the children would run to be the first in line even when he didn't give any money. I thought back to the British soldiers going into Belair with their guns, driving in their Land Rovers and how we'd think it was an honour to give them water if they stopped by our house to ask for some. I also know how I personally resented having to do that but had no understanding of why. I also thought back of the time when I threw the channa on the ground and watched the White children run and pick it up. Upon reflection, I think it was my childish attempt to take back my own power. I felt terrible for years about doing that because I was not a mean person but that day, I grabbed an opportunity and did something mean-spirited. Am I making any sense? I am not sure what I am trying to say so I think I will end this entry now and think about what I want to say a little longer.

Dear diary,

I am ready to get back to the topic of my conversation with the student. We talked for several minutes after my interview at the radio station; I put up a valiant argument as to why I was not White and I compared my skin colour with another Indian woman and rejected any similarities in skin colour with a White Canadian intern at the same centre. The student explained logically and carefully why in her appraisal, I was White. Now diary, you have to remember, this was a student who had not finished high school but her level of insight was brilliantly innocent. She was speaking from her heart and experiences and with her understanding of her world. I, on the other hand, had been teaching about White privilege and in later years, teaching about other kinds of privileges and how many of those privileges are unearned.

As a teacher-educator, I did privilege exercises with the teachers I taught in the Diversity course at Red River College and had to acknowledge my own privileges. I talked about growing up in Guyana with many privileges I never had to acknowledge because that was my lived experience. If you were: Indian, tall, light- skinned, lived a better-than-middle-income life, educated and lived in particular areas of the country, you had those privileges. No one had to explain it; you were treated differently – better. I saw it in school and I saw it in the community but I never had to acknowledge it. Diary, remember when I used to lend my rubber boots to Shanta? She was happy to wear my boots and I wanted to walk in the mud like she was doing. That was the difference between our lives; I never gave a second thought to the fact I rubber boots to lend!

I never had to think about why I had clothes for morning, afternoon, going-out and school; I never thought about the servants we had – only that we had them. I didn't have to think about the unspoken messages we somehow knew about, like not eating from someone who was Black. I didn't have to think about Neighbour being Black because to me she was just another member of my family because that's the way my parents treated her. We understood some societal messages that damned Indian women for marrying Black men and vice versa because they were marrying beneath their status but I never had to think about that. I was the Indian with the privilege of: being tall, light-skinned, living a better-than-middle-class life, having servants, having a variety of clothes for different occasions, attending a good school because my parents could afford the extra tutoring lessons to ensure that I had a better-than-average chance of getting a scholarship and an extended family who had the political, economic, cultural and social capital for a successful life.

Diary, do you know when I started to understand my life in Guyana? I arrived in Canada at 16 and for the first time in my life, I lost almost every one of those privileges I used to take for granted. Suddenly I was not fair-skinned; I was coloured. I was no taller than the average Canadian so I did not tower over the rest of the girls. I had no money and I had no social status. I lost the social, political, cultural and economic capital in one fell swoop! Many of my experiences in the 70s and early 80s were a result of losing those privileges. It was only when I entered graduate studies for the first time in the mid-90s that I could comprehend what those experiences meant.

When teaching other teachers, I talked about how I had a privileged life in Guyana and was unaware of that life; I also talked about coming to Canada – the land of opportunity – to lose almost all of it; I talked about how I had to earn those privileges over the last 40 years, but I also said that it's not enough for me to talk about privilege. It is necessary for me to go beyond talk. Based on some of the readings Chris introduced me to and some I found on my own, I read and re-read the writings of Michel Foucault about Power and how it manifests itself. Sometimes intentionally or unintentionally we exercise power over someone else or we have that power used against us overtly or covertly. It was most fascinating to read this and then use my own lenses of life to interrogate my own experiences. I could then see the power relationships at work where previously I was unable to see it. I didn't know what I didn't know but now I am gaining that awareness. I recalled reading that those with power are rarely willing to relinquish power without a fight but in my experience, it is not about conceding power. It's about making space for everyone to share in a good life.

That was my discomfort with what the student was saying to me about being White. When she and I were discussing why she thought I was White, the reasons she gave were far removed from what I understood whiteness to mean. She said whiteness to her meant I wore nice clothes that always matched and were coordinated with the appropriate colour of jewelry, I had enough food to eat each day, I had money to buy them breakfast on my way to the training centre, I came from a nice country like Canada to help them, I had had a close family because I Skyped them almost every day, I paid for all the students at the training centre to go to a game farm outside of Gaborone (some for the first time in their lives) and I taught them many things about family, friends and education. Diary, I need to leave this alone again because the more I try to explain what I want to say, the more confused I seem to get.

Dear diary,

Yes, I am back to the same conversation with the student. I tell you it's so deeply rooted in my subconscious that I feel "it" wants to take over my mind. "IT"... What is "IT"? Why is "IT" lingering so long and causing me so much confusion? What does "IT" want from me? How could a student who had not graduated from high school have taught me so much in one conversation? Whiteness to her was all about the symbols associated with someone who was part of the majority and had little or nothing to do with skin colour. I, who had taught about White privilege, was now confronted with my own identity politics in a way I had never thought about before. I mean, diary, I have always been Indian – with or without privilege – down to my core. I never questioned this until now.

Me as White meant I had to acknowledge all the privileges I also enjoyed not based on the colour of my skin but what "whiteness" represented to the student; it represented POWER. But why was I so uncomfortable with having POWER? I think it was because in many ways and for most of my life, I felt I was the one without that power, that I was living in a White culture with White people who had that power and I was far removed from access to it. I was comfortable identifying with the "other," and teaching about what it meant not to have power. In many ways, I had a privileged life and I was suddenly challenged to think of my life in a way that I had not. Having the financial capability to fund my internship in its entirety was a privilege I enjoyed that others did not.

The conversation with the student was so intensely personal that it changed my life in a palpable way. For the rest of my stay in Botswana, I started to pay careful attention to what was being said and much more to what was left unspoken or undone. Those silences said a lot. I knew by the time I left Botswana what my major paper for my master's degree would be. I had gone there to use myself as a test subject for what I thought would be my major paper on preparing students to go on intercultural or international internships. But I learned so much from the young people I met that I was no longer interested in writing about internships. A workshop I attended earlier this year on self-reflexivity resonated with me but was still a bit obscure. It became increasingly clear that, as an educator, it was not sufficient to reflect upon my actions after the fact. I had to be able to develop the ability to have ongoing dialogue with myself "in the moment" not "after the moment" and always to question my actions as well as my inactions. Diary, have I flogged this to oblivion yet? I think this experience has taught me more than I anticipated. It really is a turning point in my life because so many of my life experiences are clearer than they have ever been.

Dear diary,

It's now the end of the year and I am back in Winnipeg. The news is not good at all. Dad and Mom went back to Winnipeg after their two-week stay with me in September. I was so happy to see him doing so well after the intense 30 rounds of radiation. Dad has such an incredibly positive attitude about his life and his cancer. One of my friends who knew him since I was a teenager asked how he was doing and he said that he believed that God lifted him up and threw him down hard but God also made sure he fell on a bed of feathers so he is grateful for life. I don't know how strong I would have been in the circumstances but Dad said he would not be so strong if I was not at his side every step of the way. That's a huge responsibility to carry.

Diary, we went to his doctor for a check-up when I returned to Winnipeg after the semester ended. This was just supposed to be a routine check-up after the radiation but when the doctor did a CT scan, they found that the cancer had moved to his lymph nodes on the right side of his neck. Dr. Sathya told Dad just prior to the start of the radiation that they removed all the cancer during the surgery and the radiation was just for good measure. They did say, however, that there is a 20% chance the cancer could return and if it does so in the original site, they would not be able to do anything further for Dad. Essentially, the cancer would be terminal. Fortunately for Dad, it was not in the original place. He is scheduled for surgery at the beginning of January so I will stay until after the surgery and if it doesn't go well, I'll ask for a leave of absence from school and stay in Winnipeg until he is better. Happy Christmas and all that. That is my sarcasm and anger coming through, diary, although I don't know who to be angry with. Is there really a God and where is she when I need her? I have not been overly religious – well, not religious at all – but I am a spiritual person and I know there is some greater power than me. One turns to one's faith in times of crisis but I don't know where I should lay my prayers. Do I pray to a Hindu, Muslim or Christian God? Are they not the same? Doesn't growing up in a multi-faith home give me and my family some additional protection? I think not.

2007

Dear diary,

Another new year has arrived and Dad had his surgery. He was unbelievably brave again and only spent a few days in the hospital after another six-hour surgery. That's two major surgeries in only a few months. The doctors removed about 29 lymphatic nodules from the right side of his neck and he is healing quite well. He does not complain at all but when he has to do his exercises like lifting his arm over his head, you can see the tears involuntarily running out of his eye. I wish I could take the pain away but he would not want me to do that. Life is playing hard ball with our family and we need to dig into our reserves of strength to get through this. I came back to York to finish my studies. In December I submitted my application to the PhD program in my faculty of Environmental Studies; I think I have a good chance but I decided that if I didn't get in, then I wouldn't pursue it anymore because it wasn't meant to happen. Ray Rogers was on the selection committee and he said I was one of the strongest candidates this year. So good karma is working once again. I got in and was fully funded and I even received an entrance scholarship for my good grades.

Dad will need some more radiation but the doctors said that although they think they got all the cancer, they cannot be 100% sure so the radiation will give that added peace of mind. Dad was ecstatic about my acceptance into the PhD program. I think he's told every person who has called to wish him well. It's as if he now has a new lease on life. I'm pretty happy too because there is so much more learning I want to do.

I asked Chris Cavanagh to be my supervisor for my major paper and he agreed. He has a lot of students asking him and he is only a part-time faculty so I feel lucky that he has accepted to be my supervisor. I intend to complete this degree by the end of this semester so I can have the summer off before starting the PhD program.

Dear diary,

Do you believe in karma – that what you did in a previous life determines what this life will be? Well I do. Bad karma hit again. Or maybe life comes with good and bad karma and you have to be grateful for the good which gives you the resilience to handle the bad when it comes. It's just that it's coming so fast and furious that I am still reeling from one blow before the other one hits. I am admitted to the PhD program for the fall and I have been revelling in that for a couple of months along with Dad doing well with his surgery. The doctors were planning another set of radiation for him but decided he needed to have all his teeth removed. It got more complicated when they said that every tooth in his mouth had to be removed because they were going to radiate this right-side face and if he ever had any problems with his teeth or gums, it would be disastrous. They also said he would not be able to wear dentures for at least six months which is how long the gums would take to heal. I did not want to deal with any of it. First his eye was taken, then his teeth would have to go, then more radiation, and all this happening right as I was about to get ready for my final exam. I called my friend Barry who is a denturist and he said he would make some dentures for Dad after the extraction and after six months when the gums shrank, he would make another set. In another desperate attempt to save Dad's teeth, I called Melissa's dad who was a dental surgeon and he said that with proper dental care, Dad would be able to keep his teeth and he agreed to see Dad monthly.

The radiation was scheduled to start at the beginning of March so the doctors arranged for Dad to get casted for a radiation frame and as a precaution, they did another CT scan to make sure there was no cancer left. On March 2nd, Mom called me and said that Dr. Sathya wanted me to call him. I thought he wanted to discuss the radiation treatments but what he said felt like a horse kicked me in the head. He said the CT scan showed that Dad's cancer had returned in his eye area. Diary, that was the original area the doctors said would be problematic. There was a 20% chance it would return in the original spot but Dad was not the lucky 80%. I think I was writing down what Dr. Sathya was saying word for word but after our conversation when I looked at what I had written, it was the words "terminal," "6-18 months," "travel," "2-4 months," "tell," "pain management," "terminal," "terminal?" "Terminal." I sat for several minutes trying to replay the conversation but it would not make any sense. I was alone in an apartment on campus and what I did know for sure was that the doctor said that Dad's cancer was terminal and he asked if I wanted to tell Dad or if I wanted him to do so. I said I would. So I called my friend Prak and asked him to give me a ride to the airport the next morning. I think it was only when he asked me to slow down because he could not understand anything I was saying that I realized I was crying and incomprehensible. I calmed myself sufficiently to call Dad and we had as normal a conversation as one could have. He asked what I was going to do for the weekend and I said I would be studying.

The next day when I showed up in Winnipeg, he knew right away that something was wrong. I tried to make small talk but I think I was so fidgety which was unlike me that he sensed that it was not good news. He assumed it had something to do with his radiation but I said there would be no radiation. Then he thought it meant the cancer was gone. I guess when your life is at stake you cling to even the smallest hope, no matter how tiny. I wanted to cling to that for him but what I had to say instead was terrible. I told him the cancer had returned to the original site and it was now terminal. I'm sure if he heard me, he pretended not to or maybe he pretended not to as a way of coping with bad news. Whatever the reason, I had to say it again and at least twice more. I could feel the bile rising in my throat and felt I would not make it to the bathroom in time, but it never came. Instead I sat there with dry mouth and kept talking but I have no recollection of what I said.

Finally, I told him that he had 6-18 months so he should make the best of it. That sounded like the absolute worst thing to say; I, who could talk so much, had no adequate words for telling someone they have only six months to live but this was no ordinary someone. This was the person whose life was wrapped around mine from the day of my birth. This was the person who taught me the importance of family, explained why I had 16 grandfathers, scolded me, praised me, expected more from me than I thought I was capable of being or doing, who told me repeatedly I should stop trying to save the world, who was proud of my achievements and who told people that I am his Lakshmi. By his standards, no ordinary name would do for me. He told me my name Savitree was part of the Gayatri Mantra, the holiest and most sacred Hindu mantra and that I represented the Divine, that's why he wanted that name for me. I wanted to recite the mantra at that moment – to ask the divine mother to remove the darkness that was hanging over our heads and fill our world with brightness.

I remember this part of the conversation clearly though. After I finished with the banalities, Dad finally asked his most important questions: "But San, why me? Why did God do this to me?" I had no rational answer for my father. So instead I said: "Dad, we can do this two ways. You have cancer. You have diabetes. You can either live with cancer or wait to die from it. You have diabetes and you live with that by managing your diet and taking the right medications. So you decide. We are both fighters and as long as you are willing to fight for your life, I will be there fighting right along with you." He decided that day that he would fight and I decided the next thing I needed to do was go back to Toronto and do my exam or Dad would blame his illness on my stopping school.

Dear diary,

I passed my oral exam and decided to move back to Winnipeg at the beginning of April. The five semesters I spent at York were really very good. I learned a lot about popular education which I think I was already doing but didn't have a name for. I incorporated that into my major paper and Chris and the other committee members said it was an excellent representation of self-reflexivity. I met Celia Haig-Brown who is a professor in the Faculty of Education, and she has agreed to be on my PhD committee in the Fall when I start my studies. I met her last spring when I attended the workshop on self-reflexivity. I introduced myself and told her I was interested in doing a PhD but didn't know how I should go about doing that. She gave me some good advice and that's another reason why I applied into FES.

Mom and Dad were both excited about my acceptance into the PhD program. I remember when Dad used to tell me I can't save the world. Now he is saying he knows I can make a difference and I have to believe I should at least try. I told Dad that if he was still okay by Fall, I would start my studies but if I was more needed in Winnipeg, I would defer. He would hear nothing about me being needed in Winnipeg but I was equally determined I would defer my studies if I needed to. There was no talk of quitting – only deferring to a later date.

Dad wanted to go to Guyana so I accompanied him and Mom on a two-week trip in May. I think it may be the last time he can go so I want to make sure he does everything he wants to do. Dad wanted to have a pooja at Auntie Betty's house so he asked her to invite all our family who she could contact. There was a huge turnout and he was very happy to see his brother who arrived from England and the one who lived at De Kendren. Many of Mom's family came too so it was a reunion of sorts for the Bayney and Khan family.

I went to visit Cumming's Lodge school. Over the last few years, we raised some money through alumni events but there is still so much to do. There are several alumni who are in positions of power in the government and other organizations that can contribute or at least oversee some renovations to the school but there is this sense of indifference that frustrates me when I talked to a few of them. The computer lab we helped build is awful. It's padlocked and dusty because there is little infrastructure to support the lab. The "new" science room had not a scrap of furniture let alone equipment. The only thing evident was a piece of rolled up paper on the floor. Even the school yard that was used as a recreation area for the students was in such a state of disrepair that the students have no place to go except for the rows of food vendors selling junk food on the actual school property. I came back dispirited but still thinking that we have to do something. The students succeed in spite of the limited resources so there is so much potential for success if they have a bit more. I contacted the alumni when I returned to Canada and they committed to doing more to help but I am so far away from most of them, that most of what I do is by email or phone.

Dear diary,

It's now the beginning of September and I just started my PhD program. It was a joyous couple of weeks in August because I now have two more grandbabies – Sabreena born to Sharm and Trent and Ronin born to Sunita and Mike. That was slightly tempered by my Taiwanese friend Holly who went back to Taipei in May because she is not feeling well. She was just diagnosed with terminal cancer and the doctors have given her two months. She is not even 40 years old and she has a 14-year-old son who she named after Robin. I don't understand why the people who I love get taken from me so soon. I know this is not about me but she is such a wonderful person and because of her I learned a great deal about Chinese culture and traditions. I wanted to visit her before it's too late but I found out just a week before my grandbabies were born so I had to choose to be in Winnipeg and not see her or choose to go to Taipei and not be present for the births. I chose to stay in Winnipeg for Sabreena's birth and went to Edmonton a few days later after Ronin was born, then it was off to Toronto to settle in before school started.

I decided that if I had to be in Toronto for a few years, it was best to invest in a second home so I bought a condo but I cannot handle the Toronto traffic during rush hour so I may park my car and use public transportation. I have not done that for many years but it will free up at least 90 minutes each day to and from school. I can use every bit of time now that I have seen my schedule. I intend to work very hard and hope that Dad doesn't get worse too soon. He is doing very well and if you didn't know his cancer was terminal, you'd think he's doing well. His face is disfigured from the cancer but he has adjusted really well. We went to the optician and they designed a pair of glasses with one regular lens and one black lens with a dark side panel so that if someone was looking at him from the side, they cannot tell that he has only one eye. When he wears his sunglasses, his missing eye is hardly visible. I know how fussy he is about his appearance so I am trying to do whatever I can to make him less self-conscious. He's even joked with a child who once asked him what was wrong with his eye. He told the child he was a pirate.

2008

Dear diary,

I am into week two of my second term of my PhD studies. Last term was very hectic and sometimes I feel like I am drowning in work. Last July I got a contract from the Canadian Trucking Human Resource Council to prepare some curriculum materials and the work was supposed to be done before I started school but they delayed the project till September so I was doing that at the beginning of my studies. I thought it was a good plan when I started but when all the work started piling up, I felt like a bunny on a treadmill. It's done now but I promised myself I would not do that again. Agreeing to work on the contract was my way of earning some money beyond what my scholarship provides. Robin doesn't understand why I would be so silly about this because we can certainly afford for me to go to school. I think it goes back to my first years of marriage when I had no understanding of money because my Dad always provided for me prior to that. Then I got married and became poor – at least in my definition. I know there are many definitions of poverty but not having money to do most things I was accustomed to was poor for me. I still remember asking Robin for money to buy a $6 pair of shorts and how embarrassed I felt.

I want to earn my own money and I think that over the years I have contributed equally to our financial success so there is no logical reason for me to feel bad about spending money on my education. But I do, diary. I do. It's the need to feel independent and not to have to be accountable for how I spend what I earn. But it's more than that. It feels like I have the luxury of quitting work to go back to school and I really do; but it also means using my scholarship money to finance my education. I am not contributing to our savings account because of the salary I am not earning. So this degree is costing me financially even though the funding I get pays for my tuition and living expenses. I am not complaining about my funding but I sometimes think it's unfair I am not eligible for additional scholarships because I am not financially needy. The definition of financially needy should be reworded to mean financially destitute because I honestly don't know how some students survive on what they get. Yes, diary, in many ways, I am living a very privileged life and I do acknowledge it.

Dear diary,

It's been a very stressful two semesters. I wish I could just be a student having only to worry about my studies. I have no free time and I am constantly worrying that I am still in school and not contributing to our finances or that I am not in Winnipeg if Dad gets worse or that I am not there to support Mom. I am becoming a worrier about everything but the things I worry about are so huge, I don't know which one to disregard because they all seem equally important. I don't know why I spend so much time worrying about finances. I think as a partner in the marriage, I am obliged to contribute more than I am doing right now but Robin says that when he was young and building his career, I stayed home and took care of the children so now it's my turn. It's the guilt of being a woman of my generation, I think. We are socialized to think we are not to ask for or expect anything and we are selfish if we do anything other than what is expected. Those childhood experiences I spent so much time resisting must have influenced me anyway.

Okay, I know this is my coping mechanism taking over so I am deliberately going to leave worrying for now and tell you about this course I am auditing, a course called Feminist Perspectives. The readings make me think about how in many societies, gender roles are culture-bound and often defined by religious and cultural beliefs and expectations. Girls and women are generally the ones who are constrained by these. My own gender identity has been formed by many of my childhood experiences so that's why I think that although I contribute in other ways to the household, I worry that if it's not financial, it is not worth anything. Rationally, I know that all the years spent as a stay-at-home mom with the kids in their activities and involved in the parent-teacher associations and in community volunteering were meaningful, but society doesn't measure women's work by those measures. It has to be financial. It's surprising to me sometimes that in many ways I think of myself as a feminist and yet I can feel the guilt that often comes with that "liberation." How liberated am I if I can feel guilty for things beyond my control or for wanting an education? I've asked you so many questions. I am sure one day I'll open the page and find you have written back to me. I'm sure that you do because you allow me to tell you what I feel and it seems as soon as I give you my words, you know exactly how to soothe my soul.

Dear diary,

It's now the beginning of April and I made a difficult decision last month. I am giving up my PhD funding and going back to Winnipeg because I feel Dad needs me and I would feel better knowing that I am within minutes of his home rather than the two hours by plane that is the reality now. I'll plan to continue my studies from there but it will depend on how much time I will need to be a caregiver. It's been very stressful being a full-time student living 2,000 miles away from my family and worrying about Dad's terminal cancer. I call my parents every day but I find that having to deal with emotional issues from Toronto is too difficult without the support of my husband and family nearby. I need to be closer to them because I don't know how long Dad has left. The doctors gave him 6 to 18 months to live and it's more than 12 months already. In all this time, I have not once thought of giving up my studies because in many ways, it's what keeps me balanced – even when it's a lot of effort. I worked so hard for this, and I am happy being a student but I am concerned that my studies will be adversely affected by the stress I am dealing with. I know I'll miss the intellectual discussions and the activities on campus but emotionally, I feel I'll be better off in Winnipeg. It's hard to be the strong one in the family without sometimes feeling the need to lean on someone occasionally. I don't want to be strong. I don't want to be the one who is asked for advice and is expected to come up with an answer for every situation; I don't want to be the parent to my parents; I don't want to be the pillar of strength for the family. I just want to be ... I just want to be... I don't know what I want, but I know what I don't want anymore. I don't want to care. I don't want to feel ... just for a little while. I want to be free of the responsibilities of life. I want to not care. But I do. I do. I cannot disassociate myself from my family because they are all that I have that means anything. So this is my life, diary. And as with every challenge I have had to deal with, I will deal with this too in the best way I can.

I have already committed to teaching two courses at Red River College in the summer - Diversity and Inclusiveness and Testing and Evaluation and the D & I course at Assiniboine Community College in Brandon. The D & I one is a challenge because of the topics we cover but I really believe it is even more necessary given that there are larger numbers of Aboriginal and International students enrolled at the college. I am excited about applying some of the learning I did in the MES program. I want to introduce more popular education strategies but I also want to introduce it to faculty in a way that will make them appreciate that student success is contingent on teachers being committed to being the best teachers they can be.

That particular course has taught me a lot about being a teacher but, more importantly, students - in this case, teachers - have their biases, stereotypes and prejudices just like anyone else and they don't leave that outside the classroom. I've even had to put a note in my course outline about the controversial nature of some of the topics and that discussions should be grounded in respect for everyone's opinions which means that students can disagree with someone else's ideas but personal attacks will not be tolerated. I had to do this because of my past experience with teaching this course where I had teachers making personal attacks to me either through classroom discussion, in online course chat rooms, and in their assignments and journal entries. I'll see if this year is different. Brandon's population is far less diverse than Winnipeg's but they have a large number of new immigrants who are being brought there to work in the meat processing plant. They also have a large number of migrant farm workers who are part of the community at different times of the year so that should be an interesting perspective. I think I'll do my privilege exercise; in a group of mostly racially homogeneous people, it will be interesting to see the various privileges play out because there are many farmers and Eastern European immigrants in the Brandon area.

Dear diary,

I am glad to be back in Winnipeg. Dad is doing well and thriving. He doesn't look a bit sick except for the tumour that is now growing on his neck. It's a big lump about the size of a golf ball but it doesn't hurt, so as of now, his skin looks a bit lumpy and cottage cheesy with the smaller nodules. I spent the summer teaching and working on my comprehensive papers. I finished writing my first and second one. I had a hard time trying to decide what to focus on for my dissertation because there is so much work to do in the trades but I finally decided to focus on technical and vocational education. York University is now on strike – well, the union that represents teaching assistants and contract teachers is on strike. I am not there but the union is known for being very militant so there are a number of disturbances. There is some talk the government will legislate the union back to work. My personal experience with unions has not always been favourable but taking away the workers' right to represent themselves collectively is no good. If the union holds out for what they want, the semester will be lost. As it is, the rest of this semester is lost for sure.

2009

Dear diary,

Wow. It's been many months since I last wrote to you. I am now working as a Curriculum Consultant in the Program and Curriculum Development department at Red River College. I got the position last November and within two hours of my first day, I was asked to go to Chile to teach the Certificate in Adult

Education Foundations in College Education course to a group of Mapuche teachers in Temuco. My Spanish is only at a conversational level but I went with an RRC instructor who speaks Spanish but does not know the content of the Foundations course. I did some research prior to going so I could make the course relevant to the Chilean context. While I was preparing, I did some reading about the history of the Mapuche people and also about their continued marginalization. I also read about the Pinochet regime and how the American government had a hand in that as well. The whole of Latin America was in turmoil during the last four decades and in almost every instant, the American government was involved. In Chile, the situation was made worse by the imposition of economic policies of the Chicago School of Economics – an indoctrination couched in funding from the US government for scholars from many Latin American countries. I learned a lot about Chilean history but I also learned a lot about my own history.

Now let me tell you about my Chilean teaching experience. Red River College has a partnership with an organization in Chile called CONADI to deliver the complete Certificate in Adult Education program to a cohort of nine Mapuche teachers. The partnership is intended to help educate those teachers so that they will then have the necessary skills to live and work in their communities. It's a Train-the-Trainer program. The teachers are eager to learn but they have many challenges to overcome. Several of them had to go to Temuco from outlying communities so allowances had to be made for accommodation, transportation and other challenges they faced. I ended up with a very bad cold while I was there but they were all very helpful, even when I fell into the river at Alto Bio Bio the day before I left Chile. Yes, I had a baptism of sorts when I tripped over a long skirt I was wearing and fell into the river while I was taking a picture. As if that was not bad enough, I cut my toe in the van going back to the hotel. I came home the next day looking worse for wear with a cold and a very badly cut toe. Try wearing sandals in winter in Winnipeg. Not good. Not good at all.

Dear diary,

I went back to Chile in March to teach Course Implementation but this time I had a local translator who worked with me. After my return to Winnipeg, I was asked to grade their final project – a portfolio - which was an independent study course requiring teachers to reflect on their learning and set some goals for the future. So all together, I did three courses with the teachers. It was a great experience for me and I had an opportunity to visit each community where the teachers live and work. These were not big cities but small towns where most of the Mapuche people live and work, many in the agricultural sector. It makes me appreciate the fresh fruits and vegetables I have become accustomed to eating in the winter and it makes me wonder also about fair labour practices by huge multi-national companies doing business in Chile.

In one community, I was explaining how I was part of a successful babysitting co-op in the early 80s and suggested that this could be one model to use for some of the community members who wanted to work co-operatively. In one instance, I found out that the river running through one participant's property is privatized so she cannot use the water without permission and then has to pay for it. I'm talking about water in a river. This sounded so ridiculous that I had to ask again because I may have misunderstood what she was saying. But the others said the same thing. I take that for granted in Canada – that our rivers are still free. Or at least I think they are. We can fish or use the water without penalty. I have so much more to learn about the freedoms I enjoy and take for granted.

The teachers in Chile are all doing such remarkable work even with limited resources as is the case for many such communities. The teachers appreciated that I was from Guyana and that I could understand and relate to their politics which was in many ways similar to the Guyanese experience. Seven of the nine teachers completed the program and graduated, so that's a great success rate. The other two have only one course each to complete so I do hope they get it done soon. Each of the graduates will get two diplomas – one from Red River College and the other from the University of Atacama in Chile. That's exciting! Red River College is pursuing other such opportunities in other regions of Chile and Brazil and I hope I might get the opportunity to work with teachers from other countries. That's the value of international education I envisioned and even with some project glitches, I think it was a success and the teaching and learning will go beyond the seven graduates.

Dear diary,

The work I am doing as a curriculum consultant is very rewarding and I am very committed to the work I do with respect to quality assurance in programming at the college. My PhD studies support this role and as such my readings and writings will be directly beneficial to my work in the department. We all have our own areas of expertise so we complement each other very well. At the institutional level, I think there are some opportunities to affect change in my role as a consultant and I am still teaching in the CAE program which allows me to affect change at the classroom level. If I can just add a few more hours to each day, I can get me studies done and manage my family obligations.

Dad had to get some more radiation but he is hanging in there. It's almost two and a half years since he got his terminal diagnosis but he is still fighting hard. Dad and Mom love to come over and just sit in our sunroom listening to the mourning sounds of the doves in the backyard or watching the bunnies prancing around the garden. Last year he wanted to go to India so he and Mom, Robin and I went for three and a half weeks.

He managed quite well even though I was worried he would get sick. India was never on my list of places I had any desire to see but since Dad wanted to go, I went with him. I think he would have liked to go to the Bihar region but we were told it is not safe to go there. With the feudal system of land ownership still firmly entrenched in the culture, there are many very rich people and exponentially many more poor people. What is also still firmly entrenched in the culture is the caste system which I found harder to tolerate than the poverty which was evident in every place we visited. I left India thinking that in many ways, I was glad my ancestors went to Guyana even in difficult conditions of indentureship because as the generations pass, we are less inclined to judge people by which caste they belong to. Or maybe I found it so intolerable because I was raised in a home where my mother and father taught us to be respectful of people no matter who they are.

The only place left that's on Dad's wish list is the Panama Canal but I don't think he'll be strong enough to make that one. He and Mom had already paid for that trip just prior to getting the news about his cancer so they had to cancel it. Then they planned it again just after the first round of radiation but had to cancel again because the cancer returned for a second time. His aspiration now is to see me graduate so he can go along on his journey to the next life but that's hardly an incentive for me to finish early. Talk about being caught between a rock and a hard place. I had to switch to part-time studies at the beginning of January but I have not quit so that's good. I only need to find the time to work full-time and study full-time. Haha, that should be as easy as ending world hunger. At least I passed my first comprehensive and I am just finishing revisions to the second one. I've done most of the reading for the third so I'll organize the literature to start writing soon. I'm making some headway, albeit slow, but my studies have become my solace. That's hard for people to understand but it's a way of escaping to another world when I read and write.

Dear diary,

Two years ago, Robin turned 60 and could have retired without a penalty on his pension. He has a good supervisor now and rarely has to work overtime. Most of the people who made things difficult for him have retired. Robin comes home at supper time so that we can eat together. He travels to Edmonton a few times a year on union business and gets a chance to visit Sunita and her family. He is enjoying his work so much that he thinks he may work a few more years before retiring.

2010

Dear diary,

Well I've made it this far – much farther than I thought possible in my studies. Dad's tumour is growing quite rapidly again. He had some radiation treatments to reduce the size of the tumour which was the size of a grapefruit last fall. The tumour was growing outside of his neck so it was quite visible; it looked like an alien cling-on that was created for some science fiction movie and is unbelievably ugly and scary. It makes me realize just how destructive cancer can be. Most of the time we don't see it because it's growing internally but we can see the effects of weight loss, hair loss and general malaise. With Dad it's different. He's slowing down but it has not yet gotten the better of him. He has an incredibly strong spirit and a very positive attitude or maybe it's his way of coping with the inevitable. I don't know how I would be in that situation but I am glad I have the time to talk to him.

I've been asking Dad a lot about his childhood and he told be some terrible stories of how he and his brothers were physically abused as young men. I am also learning a lot about my paternal grandmother and how kind she was but more than anything, how much he loved her and tried to protect her when she was also being abused. I asked him to tell me about his life as a young man, how he met Mom, how they got married despite the families on both sides – Hindu and Muslim – not supporting their marriage and how difficult their first years of marriage were. I talked to him about his wishes for us and he kept reminding me that if it wasn't for my perseverance, he would not have made it this far. He is now ready to go to the Panama Canal but will not go unless I go with him and Mom. I really don't think he'll be able to go for ten days but I don't want to disappoint him so I'll make the arrangements and if it doesn't work out, then I have to believe that it has to be that way. I am teaching the Diversity and Inclusiveness course in Brandon so at the end of the course, we'll go if everything is still okay.

Dear diary,

Well Dad, Mom and I made it to the Panama Canal and back and it was a trip of a lifetime for both of them. Dad was like a little child enjoying the best Christmas present – only it was in April! We had a balcony suite and we ordered a champagne breakfast for the three of us while we sat and enjoyed the view of the locks opening and closing. He loved every moment of it and I was on stress alert because of what I had to do so he could go.

A week prior to the trip, his palliative care doctor called and told me I would have to get some training in preparation for the trip. She came over to my house and started asking a series of questions:

Did I know how to give a needle? *No.*

Did I have black towels? *Yes; Why?*

Because if Dad goes on the trip and has a bleed out, Mom will surely be traumatized if she sees white towels with blood all over and I would have to deal with her too. *Why the heck were they telling me this a week before we travel?*

Did I know what a bleed out was? *No. What is a bleed out?*

The tumour is growing right next to the artery and at any given moment can puncture it and will lead to a bleed out. *Okay, in that case, I can call the ship's doctor for help.*

You won't have that much time to call the ship's doctor for help. *How much time will I have?*

Not much. *What's not much?*

A minute or two, and he'll bleed out. *Then what?*

He'll die. *He'll die? What am I supposed to do?*

You have to give him a needle with some meds in it which will make him comfortable while he is dying. *I've never given a needle. Let me review what you're telling me: My Dad may have a bleed out because his tumour could puncture his carotid artery and he will bleed out. During this time, the blood will be squirting everywhere in the room and will flow out of his body within one or two minutes. As he is dying, I will walk over to the fridge where the meds you have given me have to be stored. I am to take out the meds and put it in a syringe which I do not know how to use and then inject him so that his body can relax as the blood is draining out of his body and while I am doing all of this, I must remember to use some black towels to blot the massive amounts of blood that will be pouring out of his body. And oh yeah, I am to make sure that my Mom is not traumatized by watching my Dad die. Do I have the scenario right? Oh yes, another little detail: I won't be able to call the doctors because they'll arrive too late. Do I now have all the details accurately?*

Yes. That's correct. Do you think you'd be able to do that? *Are you mad? Are you seriously mad? I've never even given a needle, let alone to a dying man and my FATHER no less! Are you insane?*

There is another option. *Please tell me because that was not an option. That is pure insanity and as much as I want my Dad to have this trip, I am not prepared to do that.*

The other option is to give him the meds inter-nasally. *So everything stays the same but instead of giving him a needle, I spray the meds in his nose as he dies? That's almost as ridiculous as the first option. No. I am not going to do that either.*

Well, as his doctor, I can give you a medical note to say he cannot travel so he won't be able to go on the trip. I know that this is asking a lot of you and as a medical doctor, I sometimes find it hard to do that for my patients. Let me know what you want me to do. *Now? Do I have to let you know now?*

Yes. I have to know now so I can write the letter for the insurance company.

I literally had two or three minutes to think about cancelling the trip but in the end, I reasoned that if Dad was to die on the trip, then that was his karma. Dad always believed in karma and that was what made me go ahead with the trip. So there I was, passing through US Customs and Immigration with so many different drugs for Dad that I felt that I was going to be stopped for possession of drugs. I mean some of the drugs were Fentanyl and hydromorphone and some other heavy-duty pain meds that cancer patients take regularly. A lesser man than Dad would be immobilized but he was as strong as ever. I was hyper-vigilant on the trip, so much so that by the time I returned home, I was sick for a good ten days while Dad wanted me to plan an Alaskan cruise. I told him what I was dealing with on the Panama trip and he and Mom both agreed that had they known that, they would have cancelled. I wanted him to have the trip so I said nothing until he decided he wanted another cruise. I couldn't put myself through that again. On top of being overly watch-ful, I was also getting ready for my third comprehensive exam and my dissertation proposal exam. I need to prepare for that because I want to move along with my studies.

Dear diary,

I finished my three comprehensive papers and had my dissertation proposal exam at the end of June. I am satisfied with my progress so far. My committee members guided me for the last three years and I can now use the three comprehensive papers as the first three chapters in my dissertation. Susan Hornshaw has been a tremendous help to me. I was introduced to her at the beginning of my PhD studies by my colleague Alison who thought that Susan might be a good resource and perhaps might even serve on my committee if I asked her. She has a lot of experience in both universities and colleges so she could totally relate to my research. Although I have not yet met her in person, I really value her input because she has a good grasp of what happens in colleges and we've had some good conversations about those experiences. My other committee members are Ray Rogers who is in my faculty and was my supervisor at the beginning of my studies and Celia Haig-Brown who is now my supervisor for the dissertation part. This is the same Celia who was mentioned to me a few years ago by my former professor, Laara Ftiznor. After several conversations with Celia, she agreed to serve on my committee and has been one of the most valuable assets I can have at this stage. She is extremely knowledgeable about adult education so once again, I feel fortunate to have such a strong committee.

I finally received my ethic approval from York University to conduct a series of focus groups with instructors at RRC but I need to get the same from RRC. I hope that comes soon and I can get on with the rest of my dissertation. The last two weeks have been incredibly stressful. Dad's condition is rapidly deteriorating and I'm being pulled in every direction right now. I may not be writing you for some time but you have always been there for me and I know you'll continue to be there when I need you.

By the way, someone sent me a link to a BBC documentary about the events of Guyana in the 1960s. It's interesting to listen to it because through extensive research to prepare the documentary, the research team uncovered extensive evidence that the United States and Britain were directly implicated in the events of those days. I am sure it changed the course of many people's lives in Guyana and makes me even more aware that things shouldn't be taken at face value, even or especially, the education we received. Education is political and someone needs to speak for the dispossessed. I think I'll title my dissertation to read something like that. In this case, the dispossessed are the vocational students and teachers who are so often marginalized and live in the borderland of education.

There is so much research on vocational education but much of it is quantitative and focuses on how many students graduate and how many find jobs. Qualitative research is not generally done in vocational education and I want my research to focus on how teachers deal with the challenges of teaching in a college where they are hired as subject matter experts and are asked to teach with no teacher training. In vocational education, we ask the most underprepared teachers to teach the most underprepared students and expect fantastic results. By some marvel, many of the students succeed but almost as many leave school without completing their studies. We don't seem to worry about those "early leavers" because they go off to fend for themselves in whatever job they end up with or if they are motivated enough, will enrol in another program.

2011

Dear diary,

I have neglected you terribly. It has been quite a busy and stressful year. Juggling family responsibilities with full-time work and almost full-time studies has almost overtaxed my planning and time management skills. A lot has happened in the last few months but at least the events have not completely derailed my studies. Since I am using RRC as my case study for my dissertation, I had to apply to RRC's ethics board for approval to conduct research with the vocational teachers. I finally received the ethics approval in late November with the condition that I was not to be directly involved in conducting the focus groups with the teachers at the college because the ethics review committee was concerned that because I work at the college, I may at some future date be in a potential power relationship with the instructors and may use that power in a negative way. I agreed to their conditions and had someone lined up to conduct the focus groups in January. By the end of February when I did not get a response from the facilitator, my friend Brent recommended a friend who was experienced at conducting focus groups. After meeting and chatting with Irene in early March, I knew she was the one. That's me relying on my intuition and it pays off every time.

At the beginning of February, well, the day before my birthday, Dad had a big bleed and we had to take him to the Riverview Health Centre. He hated that place. I don't often use the word "hate" but he detested the facility and only wanted to go home. That's where we spent his 80th birthday. I made him promise a few days prior that he was not going to be sick for our birthdays so he apologized that he ended up bleeding and had to be hospitalized. I was only joking about his not getting sick but I am glad he reached his 80th birthday. It's been a struggle for him in the last few months. He had another round of radiation which really took a toll on him and he ended up hospitalized because of severe dehydration. Dad and Mom have been getting about 22 hours of home care each day since November. I have become a fiendish advocate for their health and wonder how people manage who do not have an advocate as they navigate a sick health care system. I managed to get him transferred to the Grace Hospice only a week after he went to the Riverview; the place is beautiful but he still wanted to go home. A few days after he went there he needed round-the-clock medical care; I felt very guilty about that but there was no more we could do for him at home. Mom is also getting tired and having to worry about both of them is beyond stressful for me.

Irene agreed to conduct a focus group in March and another one in April. After they were done, I talked to Dad about them and he was pretty happy that I was again making progress with my studies, He kept reminding me he was proud of my success and that he foresaw great things in my future. He also reminded me that he wanted to see me graduate. I felt the pressure but reminded him again that my studies were for me, not for anyone else – not even him – but I was grateful for all he taught me about the importance of family, including those who came before us to Guyana in difficult circumstances and how hard they worked so future generations could have a better life than they did.

Dear diary,

My race against time is over. Dad passed away just days after my second focus group was completed. After that, Irene was kind enough to offer to collect information from an online survey asking the same questions as the focus group questions. She's been a huge help because the last thing I could cope with was my studies.

While Dad was in the hospice, Mom moved in with us and just before Dad passed, their house was sold. With trying to get her settled into our home, dealing with funeral arrangements, selling their house and furniture and transferring all the relevant documents regarding benefits, insurance, pensions and bank accounts on her behalf, I did nothing with my studies until early July. I had set a schedule for the completion of my studies for August, but with all the delays in ethics approval, focus group facilitation, Dad's passing and settling Mom into her new life, I have been stressing myself out about how to get my work done. At the beginning of July, I finally ploughed right in and had that done within six weeks. The instructors had a lot of useful things to say about their teaching experiences which were mostly similar to mine. I am looking forward to doing the analysis of the data but there are so many thoughts going around in my head that I can't seem to focus on what I need to say. I think I have to write it down so I can see it on paper.

I often find myself lying in bed at night thinking of what the end of the dissertation might mean for me and whether the findings will make any difference. I have to believe that if it doesn't in the immediate future, it will at a later date. I also wonder what it might mean for my career if some of the findings are not favourable for the college. I cannot yet envision a future without Dad and without my studies. That's been my life for the last five years. Dad mentioned many times that he thinks I should write a book about my life's experiences but right now, I just want to be done with my studies. I have so many other things I want to do, that I may finally find the time to do them. I spent the last three decades documenting my family tree so I would like to do something about turning it into a book or some resource for my family. The family tree started out being a family tree but over three decades, it's turned into a family jungle with many shoots growing in different directions. It's so interesting how you unearth secrets and stories you were never told before when you are documenting family history. Some of them are wonderful and worth sharing because learning about our past makes us stronger as we look to our future.

Dear diary,

It is now a few days after Christmas and I have sent off my final chapter to Celia. It has been a very hectic time this month. With work and writing pretty much every day and most weekends this month, I am mentally drained. I feel I have finally put in writing much of what I have been living in the last three decades. It feels like my life has been leading to this but I still feel there is so much more left to do. I have been asked a number of times in the last few months about my plans for the future and what I am going to do when I've completed my studies. I have not really given much thought to that because I've never really thought of the dissertation as the end of anything. It is indeed a milestone but I think that in spite of the challenges of working and studying in technical/vocational education, I think my experiences have made me who I am. I am looking forward to the next stage of my life, whatever it brings. I'll let you know how my exam goes and I want to thank you for always being a faithful and patient friend.

I was not ready to celebrate Christmas the way we've done with my parents over the last three decades –at my home for Christmas lunch – so Robin and I, Sharm and her family, Sunita and her family, Subhadra and Mom rented a house in Orlando for two weeks and enjoyed a green Christmas. It was different but I am happy we came and I am looking forward to the new year. When I submitted my last chapter, I told Celia I want to be done by next April. I don't know what 2012 will bring but I am hopeful it will be good.

2012

Dear diary,

It is now two months into this year and I now have an exam date for my oral defence of my dissertation. It's set for April 4 and will be in Toronto. It's almost the end of this four-and-a-half-year journey of scholarship and learning and although I am looking forward to the completion of this part of my studies, I am wondering what I will do next. Family and friends keep asking if the dissertation was the final destination. If I look at my life in that way, it would mean that everything I have done till now was not important or had no meaning, but in my lifetime, I have learned so much and still feel like I have a lot more to learn. I've also learned that the path of my life is hardly predictable so whatever comes next will unfold how it is meant to.

I do hope the recommendations in the dissertation will have some meaning but even if no other person picks it up and does anything else with it, I will continue to do all I can for teachers, and ultimately, for students. I have to believe in the goodness of humankind because that will make the work I do have some meaning. Every person can make a difference – however small – and together we really can change the world – one person at a time.

Dear diary,

Today is April 19 and it is exactly one year since Dad passed away. It could be a sad day but I have decided to reframe this day as a celebratory one. I had my exam two weeks ago on April 4 and I passed. I was asked to do some very minor revisions which I did in the last two weeks and by some serendipitous act, I submitted my final version today to the Faculty of Graduate Studies. I can officially call myself Doctor but it seems rather anticlimactic. There is no fanfare, no bells ringing or no sighs of relief that I am finally done. Maybe that'll come later. Right now, I have work to catch up on. I've thought of some things I could do but for now, I'll give myself a few weeks of rest and relaxation – after I finish remodelling my kitchen, and then my life will be quiet. I don't know who I think I am kidding. My life has always been lived in overdrive so why should the next two or three decades be any different? I may do what many people have suggested over several years and write that book that's been percolating in my head for decades. I know Dad would have been very proud of my achievements as he always believed I would do this, but more to the point, I know there is so much to learn and do that I will continue the fight for all those people who believe a better world is possible.

Dear diary,

It's the end of the year and we have just celebrated Christmas as has been our tradition for the last three decades except that Dad was not at the table. This year it was much easier to listen to the Nat King Cole Christmas carols Dad loved to sing. This time of year is always special because it reminds me of my childhood and the traditions we had on Christmas Eve when Dad would take us window-shopping downtown and give us some money to buy Christmas presents for each other. It is also a time for me to see the future in my grandchildren and hope as they grow up, I can tell them about their great- and great-great-grandparents. I want them to know their ancestry and how blessed they are to have ancestors and family who come from several continents and experiences and are making a life together. I am also doing what I have wanted to for many years - write that book that tells the story. I've decided on the title of the book: *In Search of the Blue Lotus*.

Diary, you have been the most faithful friend to me since I was a little girl. You have never judged me as a girl, rich, poor, hairstylist, teacher, teacher-educator, mother, wife, daughter, sister, friend or any other label I can think of for myself or that someone else has given me. If only the world was like you. You see, diary, this book is less about me and more about what those labels represent. We are all given labels that can either bind us or set us free. You need to tell my story which is not really my story but the story of every person. Whether you are a man or woman, rich or poor, educated or not, this is your story. It is the counter-narrative that must be told so that we can work towards a transformative future for all.

Afterword

In several cultures, the lotus flower is greatly significant. Growing up with many Hindu relatives, I understood the significance of the lotus as sacred. My Dad used to tell me that the lotus flower (sometimes called water lily) was the most sacred flower. Several deities either sat on or held a lotus flower. The flower grows in dirty water but never seems to be touched by the dirtiness of its surroundings.

As a young girl, I used to go into the dirty water to pick the flowers as if fascinated by them. Sometimes I would break open the flower to eat the tiny nuts inside; other times I would bring them home simply to stare at them. I can still feel the texture of the leaves as smooth and soft as if they were powdered. The pink tips would fade into paler shades of pink until they met the yellow centres. The leaves are bowl shaped, perfect for use at many Hindu weddings long before the environment was a concern for many. I ate many a meal at Hindu weddings and other religious functions of rice, dhall, puri and various curries. Eaten in a lotus leaf, food has a special taste of the essential oil of the leaf blended with the hot food. It makes me have wonderful memories of special family events.

It would seem apropos at this time that I should find in the lotus flower, the perfect symbol of what this book means to me. In researching the symbolism of the lotus flower, I found that the flower gained more significance as I connected it to the Gayatri mantra - the most sacred Hindu prayer – and to my name Savitree, which is another representation of the Gayatri mantra. Savitri (pronounced Savitree) sits on a lotus leaf and represents knowledge and help to mankind. Co-incidentally, my name Sandra means the same thing – helper of mankind. Each colour of lotus flower had a different meaning. The blue lotus is rare and signifies mankind aspiring to a higher spiritual plane.

The Blue Lotus in this book is a metaphor for my life. The book cover illustrates blue lotus flowers in several stages of opening, symbolizing various stages of our spiritual awakening. Metaphorically, the flowers represent the aspects of our search for life's meaning. Each day we arise and start our day hopeful, as does the lotus flower, in a world full of contradictions - of beauty and ugliness. Each day we try to see the goodness in each other and find that sometimes we are not as virtuous as we would like to be but at the end of the day, we make a promise to be better than we were the day before. We'll fail and we'll succeed but we cannot stop trying. This book is that journey of self-awareness. The stories are less about me and more about what we have in common. It is my hope that one or more of the diary entries will resonate with you and regardless of my flaws, you can envision a better world for all – as I do each day.

Bibliography

(Endnotes)

1 Reed-Danahay, D. E. (Ed.). (1997). Auto/*Ethnography: Rewriting the self and the social*. Berg Publishing. Oxford, UK.

2 Ellis, C., & Bochner, A. P. (2000). Autoethnography, personal narrative, reflexivity: Researcher as subject. *In* N. K. Denzin & Y. S. Lincoln (Eds.), *Handbook of qualitative research* 2nd ed., pp. 733-768. Sage Publications, Thousand Oaks, CA.

3 Spry, T. (2001). Performing autoethnography: An embodied methodological praxis. *Qualitative Inquiry*, 7(6), 706-732.

4 Wexler, P. (1996). *Holy sparks: Social theory, education, and religion*. New York: St. Martin's Press.

5 Kincheloe, Joe L.. (2002) *Teachers as Researchers : Qualitative Inquiry as a Path to Empowerment* (2nd Edition). London, GBR: Falmer Press.

6 Svensson, Birgitta (1997). The Power of Biography: Criminal Policy, Prison Life, and the Formation of Criminal Identities in the Swedish Welfare State. Chapter 3 In *Auto/ Ethnography: Rewriting the self and the social*. Berg Publishing.

7 Heider, Karl G. (1988). The Rashomon Effect: When Ethnographers Disagree. *American Anthropologist*, New Series, Vol. 90, No. 1. March, pp. 73-81